ROUTLEDGE LIBRARY EDITIONS: HIGHER EDUCATION

Volume 1

THE BUSINESS OF HIGHER EDUCATION

THE BUSINESS OF HIGHER EDUCATION
The American University and its Banking Function

NOAM H. ARZT

LONDON AND NEW YORK

First published in 1995 by Garland Publishing, Inc.

This edition first published in 2019
by Routledge
2 Park Square, Milton Park, Abingdon, Oxon OX14 4RN

and by Routledge
52 Vanderbilt Avenue, New York, NY 10017

Routledge is an imprint of the Taylor & Francis Group, an informa business

© 1995 Noam H. Arzt

All rights reserved. No part of this book may be reprinted or reproduced or utilised in any form or by any electronic, mechanical, or other means, now known or hereafter invented, including photocopying and recording, or in any information storage or retrieval system, without permission in writing from the publishers.

Trademark notice: Product or corporate names may be trademarks or registered trademarks, and are used only for identification and explanation without intent to infringe.

British Library Cataloguing in Publication Data
A catalogue record for this book is available from the British Library

ISBN: 978-1-138-32388-9 (Set)
ISBN: 978-0-429-43625-3 (Set) (ebk)
ISBN: 978-1-138-33039-9 (Volume 1) (hbk)
ISBN: 978-1-138-33042-9 (Volume 1) (pbk)
ISBN: 978-0-429-44790-7 (Volume 1) (ebk)

Publisher's Note
The publisher has gone to great lengths to ensure the quality of this reprint but points out that some imperfections in the original copies may be apparent.

Disclaimer
The publisher has made every effort to trace copyright holders and would welcome correspondence from those they have been unable to trace.

THE BUSINESS OF HIGHER EDUCATION

THE AMERICAN UNIVERSITY AND ITS BANKING FUNCTION

NOAM H. ARZT

GARLAND PUBLISHING, INC.
NEW YORK & LONDON / 1995

Copyright © 1995 Noam H. Arzt
All rights reserved

Library of Congress Cataloging-in-Publication Data

Arzt, Noam H., 1961–
    The business of higher education : the American university and its banking function / Noam H. Arzt.
        p.   cm. — (Financial sector of the American economy)
    Includes bibliographical references and index.
    ISBN 0-8153-2241-0 (alk. paper)
    1. Universities and colleges—United States—Business management. 2. Education, Higher—United States—Finance. 3. College costs—United States. 4. Banks and banking—United States I. Title. II. Series.
LB2341.93.U6A79 1995
378'.02'0973—dc20

                                                  95-37226

Printed on acid-free, 250-year-life paper
Manufactured in the United States of America

To Heidi Lynn

Contents

List of Tables	ix
List of Figures	xi
Foreword	xv
Preface	xvii
1. Introduction	3
2. Models of Student Price Sensitivity	23
3. Student Price Sensitivity: Results from Three Schools	51
4. Banking Functions	79
5. The Academic Bank	97
6. Case Study: The Academic Bank at PMU	115
References	141
Index	149

Tables

Chapter 2

2.1 - Statistics on High-PSAT COFHE Students, 1987   31

2.2 - Aid Estimate for a Single Student   46

2.3 - Aid Estimate for Entire Entering Class   46

2.4 - Institutional Self-assessment of Price Sensitivity   47

Chapter 3

3.1 - Differences in Yield Percentage, PMU   53

3.2 - Differences in Yield Percentage, PLA.   54

3.3a - Differences in Yield Percentage, PUC Non-residents   54

3.3b - Differences in Yield Percentage, PUC Residents   55

3.4a - Average Total Aid for PMU, by Quintile   61

3.4b - Average Total Need for PLA, by Quintile   61

3.4c - Average Total Aid for PUC Non-state Residents, by Quintile   62

3.4d - Average Total Aid for PUC State Residents, by Quintile   62

3.5a - Average Amount of Self Help for PMU, by Quintile   65

3.5b - Average Amount of Self Help for PUC Non-state Residents, by Quintile   66

3.5c - Average Amount of Self Help for PUC State
Residents, by Quintile   66

3.6a - Average Proportion of Total Aid Award that is
Self Help for PMU, by Quintile   69

3.6b - Average Proportion of Total Aid Award that is
Self Help for PUC Non-state Residents, by Quintile   69

3.6c - Average Proportion of Total Aid Award that is
Self Help for PUC State Residents, by Quintile   69

3.7 - Aggregate Difference in Total Aid Between
Admits and Matrics   71

3.8 - Aggregate Difference in Self Help Between
Admits and Matrics   72

3.9 - Aggregate Difference in Grant Between
Admits and Matrics   72

3.10 - Summary of Results from Actual Data   73

3.11 - Summary of Data as Compared to Institutional
Perception   75

Chapter 6

6.1 - Interview List for PMU Case Study   116

6.2 - Financial Aid Summary for PMU   118

6.3 - Enhanced Financial Aid Summary for PMU   118

6.4 - Current Bank-like Functions at PMU   122

6.5 - Aggregate Aid Levels for Segments of the Aided
Population of PMU, 1992   135

Figures

Chapter 1

1.1 - Average Tuition and Fees at Private U.S. Colleges and Universities — 4

1.2 - Projected Change in Private College Price, 1990 through 2010 — 4

1.3 - Average Annual Real Change in College Costs, 1978 through 1986 — 7

1.4 - Average Annual Real Change in Aid by Category, 1978 through 1986 — 10

1.5 - State Bond and Prepayment Programs — 13

Chapter 2

2.1 - Graph of Percentage Change in Proportions Within Three Broad Income Groups, 1978 to 1989 — 30

2.2 - Graph of Statistics on High-PSAT COFHE Students, 1987 — 31

2.3 - Differences in Yield Percentage — 36

2.4 - Differences in Yield Percentage Between Needy Admits with Correct Awards, Needy Admits with Incorrect Awards, and Full-paying Admits — 37

2.5a - Proportion of Population of Admits by Student Category — 38

2.5b - Proportion of Population of Matrics by Student Category — 38

2.6 - Yield by Quintile of Aid	40
2.7 - Difference in Aid Between Admits and Matrics Across the Population	41
2.8 - Ratio of Total Aid, Admits to Matrics	42
2.9 - Difference in Amount of Self Help Between Admits and Matrics	43
2.10 - Ratio of Amount of Self Help, Admits to Matrics	44
2.11 - Difference Between Admits and Matrics in the Proportion of Total Aid Award that is Self Help	44

Chapter 3

3.1 - Differences in Yield Percentage	56
3.2a - Proportion of Population by Student Category	57
3.2b - Proportion of Population by Student Category (continued)	58
3.3 - Yield by Quintile of Aid	60
3.4 - Difference in Average Total Aid Between Admits and Matrics	63
3.5 - Ratio of Total Aid, Admits to Matrics	64
3.6 - Difference in Amount of Self Help Between Admits and Matrics	67
3.7 - Ratio of Amount of Self Help, Admits to Matrics	68

Figures

3.8 - Difference Between Admits and Matrics in the
    Proportion of Total Aid Award that is Self Help   70

Chapter 4

4.1 - Types of Financial Services Institutions.   82

Chapter 5

5.1 - Academic Bank Functions and Banking Structures   98

5.2 - Banking Functions and Academic Bank Functions   100

Chapter 6

6.1 - PMU Prepayment Plans: New Dollars   124

6.2 - PMU Prepayment Plans: New Participants   125

6.3 - Increase in Price of Tuition and Fees at PMU   126

6.4 - Differences in Yield Percentage at PMU   127

6.5 - Stafford Loan Amounts at PMU   128

6.6 - Number of Stafford Loan Borrows at PMU   129

Foreword

When Noam Arzt began his study in the summer of 1989, the old world of student financial aid was still recognizable. The dual focus of financial aid was on "needs analysis," which by then had become a meta religion complete with its own icons, ideology, and intransigence, and the myriad of crisscrossing programs and regulations that comprised federal student aid. The genesis of the study, however, was a different set of questions. Noam was part of a team assisting a medical school that sought to better understand how it spent its own scholarship funds. The school approached the problem by examining whether it was making the best use out of the federal funds that were available to its students, and exploring whether a different kind of financial aid policy might make the school more attractive to its most competitive applicants. What he came to see then, and later brought to his analysis of how three undergraduate institutions distributed loan and scholarship funds, was that the institution ought to think of itself as a bank—a source of both capital and services essential to a student's successful completion of his or her education.

That was the first of Noam's three insights. The second was the increasing rate at which undergraduate institutions were discounting their tuitions. We all know now what Noam first understood then. For private institutions discounting has become the most important and often the most debilitating financial issue of the 1990's. For example, it is not at all uncommon for private institutions to be aiding, or providing discounts to, more than eighty percent of their students. Such institutions regularly find themselves giving back 35-40 cents of every tuition dollar in the form of a discount and seeing more than 75 cents out of every dollar of tuition increase consumed by the financial aid budget.

Noam's third insight was that there is a key relationship between financial aid, the need for discounts, and the attractiveness of the institution to the students it most wants to enroll. Reading *The Business of Higher Education: The American University and Its Banking Function* it becomes clear that the distribution of financial aid/discounts can be managed in such a way as to yield not only a bigger, but in at least some respects a better first year class. The implications of this insight are troubling—the idea that financial aid is transformed from a means of reducing or eliminating financial barriers to enrollment to a marketing tool that can help ensure an institution's survival. In this recast equation, the financial aid budget becomes an institutional resource rather than a means of ensuring equal access to all students regardless of ability to pay.

Thus *The American University and Its Banking Function* both contributes to and documents just how much the world of college pricing has changed over the last decade; how each of our colleges and universities has changed given that market forces increasingly shape institutional aspirations. The prospects are for more of the same: more competition based on net price, more reductions in public funds for scholarships and loans, and more need for alternative approaches for the awarding of both need-based and merit aid. Some will see in *The American University and Its Banking Function*'s compelling evidence that it is time to turn back the clock, to reaffirm that the sole purpose of financial aid is to guarantee educational access for those least able to pay the full cost of an undergraduate education. Others will see in Noam's analysis a sign of hope—an important first step in a process that will allow institutions to recast their student financial aid programs and offices, making them more business-like, more willing to experiment with new forms of financial assistance, and finally, to use Noam's frame of reference, more bank-like. Whatever perspective the reader adopts, *The American University and Its Banking Function* helps set the stage for truly important campus-wide discussions.

Dr. Robert Zemsky
University of Pennsylvania
July, 1995

Preface

What a turbulent time for higher education! As businesses strive to be more productive and more efficient through re-engineering and downsizing, so, too, are colleges and universities looking for ways to be more productive. More and more the focus is on the customer—students as customers, faculty as customers, parents as customers, alumni as customers.

This book focuses on innovation in the area of student financial services. While the study was conducted against the backdrop of the early 1990's, as we pass the half-way point of the decade of the nineties its message remains just as relevant: banking functions are a powerful tool for colleges and universities to use to meet the market's demand for new services, and are a necessary resource in an institution's "bag of tricks" to balance the ever-constrained financial aid budget. Our future is not yet cast in stone: a Republican Congress has threatened to reduce the size of and change the character of Federal aid by cutting programs and eliminating interest subsidies, while direct lending by colleges and universities appears off to a good, but uncertain, start. And there is renewed talk about providing additional incentives to save for college.

The financial services industry is undergoing its share of changes as well. The deregulation of the banking industry appears unstoppable, as mergers continue across the country and commercial banks are now starting to enter the stock and bond underwriting business. The IRS has finally abandoned its attempt to tax the State of Michigan's prepaid tuition plan (the threat alone was enough to kill its share of innovative state- and institution-based alternatives). And in an interesting twist, the College Savings Bank has recently filed a patent infringement suit against its state-run competitors to protect what it believes it to be *its* intellectual property—the formula by which future tuition is projected and used as the basis for its investment alternatives.

Use this book as a guide for thinking critically about the opportunities within your own college or university, or to help you understand some of the possibilities that might be called upon in increasingly challenging times. Consider the role of price in student decision-making, and the effects of different price discounts on student matriculation. The models presented here are meant to be tested and experimented upon. Feel free to share your results!

I would like to thank my family for all its encouragement, my mother for her careful reading early on, my father for his constant interest and support, and of course my wife, Heidi Lynn, for her never-ending patience and devotion to whatever I attempt.

Noam Arzt
arzt@isc.upenn.edu
July, 1995

The Business of
Higher Education

I
Introduction

A critical issue facing students and their families in the 1990's is the affordability of a college education. The 1989 annual rating of colleges and universities by *U.S. News and World Report* celebrated the price of a college education as the single most troublesome problem to both those on and off the college campus.[1] Increases in tuition at many colleges and universities continue to outstrip the annual rate of inflation. While at least half of the market for higher education is made up of non-traditional students, for many colleges and universities their traditional eighteen to twenty-five year old market remains intact. How can the "baby boomer" generation ever hope to be able to afford the kind of education for their children that their parents were able to provide them?

The Price of Higher Education

Perhaps most worrisome to parents and their families is the rise in the price of higher education, especially in the early 1990's when inflation has been kept low and the consumer price index continues to stay under 3%. Figure 1.1 displays the average tuition and fees for all U.S. private colleges for the past five years. The rate of increase, though slowed, continues to be more than double the rate of inflation!

In an attempt to examine future trends in college affordability, McPherson and Schapiro prepared a simulation of the change in price of attendance (defined as tuition and fees plus average living expenses, with an adjustment for non-tuition revenue on a per-student basis) for the period from 1990 through 2010. The results are shown in Figure 1.2.

They projected a significant increase in the real price of attendance, with the results being most dramatic for the private colleges and universities.[2] A variety of additional simulations were also performed based on these trends and other sets of assumptions to help predict what the actual price and aid levels might be. Most significantly, their simulation showed the extreme vulnerability that education has to a prolonged recession, as well as the favorable effect of sustained overall economic growth.[3]

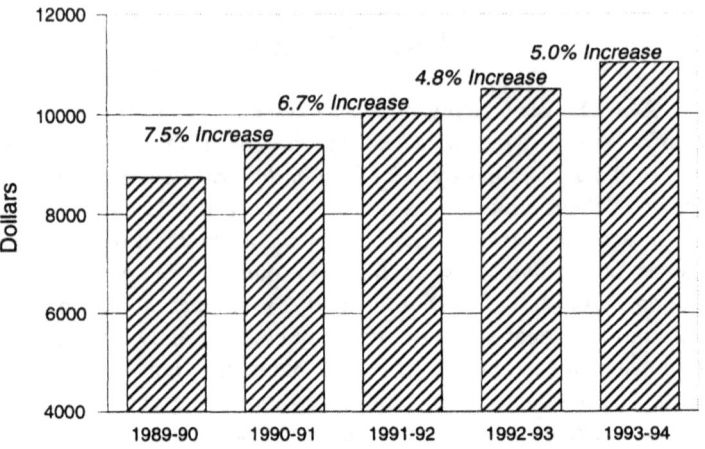

Figure 1.1 - Average Tuition and Fees at Private U.S. Colleges and Universities[4]

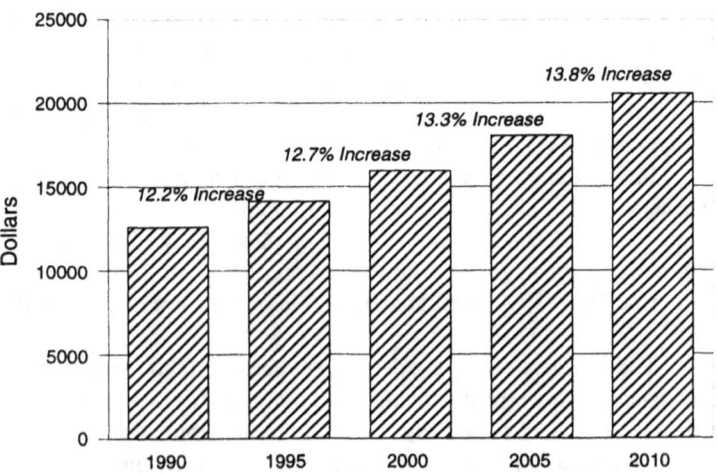

Figure 1.2 - Projected Change in Private College Price, 1990 through 2010 (in constant 1989 dollars)

The Cost of Higher Education

Since many colleges and universities continue to practice "cost plus pricing," the rate of tuition is a function of the amount (or cost) the college or university feels it expends to provide the education plus as additional margin. This creates a strong link between the perceived *cost* of a college education and the *price* charged to its customers.

Institutions are under increasing pressure to tighten their belts just at a time when enrollments in many institutions flatten, and even decline. Most, if not all, private colleges and universities are tuition driven in that they rely on income from tuition and fees to cover a substantial portion of their operating budgets (the cost of providing educational services and research). Public institutions are under pressure of their own coming off the recession of the early 1990's (which is still running strong in some regions of the country) as states try to reduce expenditures across the board and to higher education especially.

Why is the amount spent by colleges and universities to provide an education (college cost) continuing to rise so dramatically? Some studies have shown that even in a period of steady enrollments and no increases in faculty or staff size, expenses escalate faster than the rate of inflation.[5] A study by Tufts University in the late 1980's identified some important reasons why college costs continue to rise so quickly. Six general trends were identified: neglected requirements for plant upkeep and renewal; strong pressure to maintain real growth in faculty salaries; significant increases in costs for equipment and laboratories; extreme escalation in the cost for library materials; federal aid cutbacks; and costs associated with increasing regulation. Additionally, three other trends were identified as being, in the opinion of the authors, more characteristic of Tufts than necessarily all similar institutions (though they certainly hold true for many colleges and universities). They were: inadequate revenue growth from sources other than tuition; staff and faculty growth; and a general stabilization of enrollments.[6]

A whole host of other reasons can be added to the list: rising energy costs, surging benefits costs in a labor-intensive industry, and the elimination of mandatory retirement. William F. Massy, a leading researcher and former vice president for finance at Stanford University, summarizes these fundamental problems by identifying a number of common phenomena. "Cost disease" is the tendency for costs in institutions of higher education to rise faster than inflation even when enrollments and faculty size do not. "Growth force" is a phenomenon that forces budgets to increase as institutions create new programs without discontinuing old ones. The overall expense pie gets bigger rather than the slices changing size with respect to one another. Massy's primary focus is on the problems higher education has in increasing productivity, both in the academic and administrative support services areas, and how various factors provide obstacles to improvement: build-up of organizational slack with no ways to consume it in lean times, accretion of unnecessary tasks that seem to develop lives of their own, and function lust, which has administrative units competing with each other rather than working together towards common goals.[7]

The evidence of some of these phenomena is becoming clear. Data collected by the U.S. Equal Opportunity Employment Commission from 3,300 institutions show that professional support staff overall grew at the rate of 4.5% from October 1990 to October 1991. While this was less than the 7% growth rate from 1975 to 1980, it is nonetheless significant. Faculty grew by only 1.2% from 1990 to 1991.[8] And the effects are beginning to hurt. In 1991-92, almost half of all public four year institutions reported that their budgets either stayed the same or declined, up from 36% the previous year. Only 14% of the independent institutions had budgets either cut or stay the same in either 1990-91 or 1991-92,[9] though 35% of them expect a budget cut in 1992-93.[10] Funding cuts at state universities are particularly severe, often producing tuition increases of as much as 40%.[11]

As a basis for part of their simulation, McPherson and Schapiro calculated the real change in the cost of higher education (education and general expenditures on a per student basis) for the years 1978 through 1986. The average change in cost is displayed in Figure 1.3.[12]

By controlling costs, colleges and universities should be able to bring the rate of change in the price of attendance closer to the rate of inflation. Accomplishing this is no easy feat, however. Simply slashing budgets will not solve these long-term problems; rather "those who are inclined to put higher education on a diet in order to curb its appetite should understand that the most likely result will be thinner rather than healthier institutions."[13]

Introduction

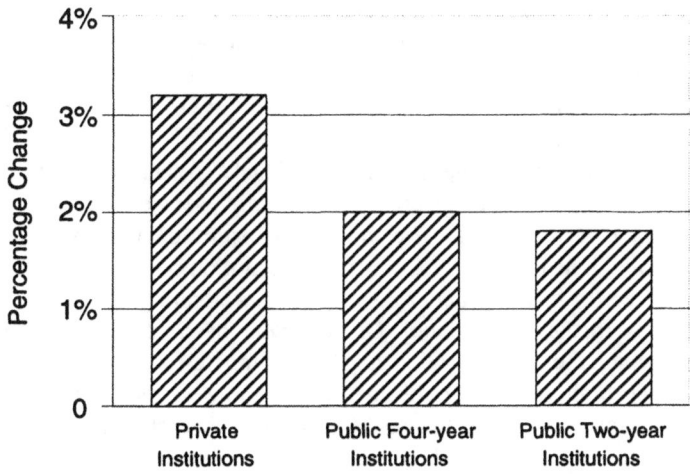

Figure 1.3 - Average Annual Real Change in College Costs, 1978 through 1986

Net Price and Price Sensitivity

When it comes to college choice, institutions are learning that price is a major factor in a student's application and matriculation decisions. College is expensive, and many families are not able to afford the full price.[14] Individual institutions are beginning to recognize the market forces to which they are subject: prospective students, with incomplete information, are making choices at least in part based on price. How an institution sets its price can create a condition known as price sensitivity. By this it is meant simply that other things being equal, a prospective student will matriculate at the institution that offers the lowest price and place less significance on other factors such as the academic merits or the overall experience offered by the college or university.

Several effects become evident. When examining college recruitment material, some students and their families experience "sticker shock" when they read the published, full price of attending some colleges and universities. If they allow fear of paying this full price to affect their decision to apply or matriculate, then they are price sensitive. In fact, many students and their families do not pay the full, published price of attendance, but rather receive one of several kinds of price discounts. The full ("sticker") price less the discount yields a *net price* of attendance. It is a student's sensitivity to the net price of attendance that warrants more close attention.[15]

One important note needs to be made. When an institution perceives that its applicants are becoming price sensitive, one of two things may be happening. The individual institution may have set a price too high in its market. Competing institutions may be charging a lower price (or offering better discounts) and affecting the decision of applicants in the mutual pool. On the other hand, the entire market within which the institution and its peers compete for students may be priced too high, leading applicants to look more seriously at colleges and universities in other (ostensibly cheaper) markets. An individual institution may not know which of these effects is taking place.

Initial Discounts to Price: Financial Aid

For many students, need-based financial aid has provided the single greatest discount to the price of attending college. For an increasing number of students, merit-based financial aid may start to play an important role. The dramatic change in the price of higher education over the past ten years has been matched by a dramatic change in the makeup of the financial aid discount. An ever-increasing proportion of the bill for attending college is being paid for by funds received in the form of loans. In addition, loans have increased dramatically as a proportion of total aid. While in the mid-1970's loans accounted for approximately 20% of all student aid, by the start of the 1980's they had increased to over 40%.[16] By the end of the 1980's this percentage soared to over 50%.[17]

Stafford loans are the best example, and have become the most popular and readily available form of self-help. Increasing default rates, as well as abuses by proprietary schools and others, have caused Congress to threaten to reduce the availability of funds through this program. Congress has considered legislation to limit the eligibility of part-time students for Pell grants,[18] another cornerstone of the federal financial aid program, and Stafford loans may be next. As the profile of many college students shifts away from that of traditional, four-year, post-high school matriculants to older, often part-time, students,[19] these new limits on federal financial aid will have a strong impact on these students' ability to pay for attendance.

Overall, financial aid at the Federal level has not kept up with inflation. From academic year 1980-81 to academic year 1986-87, total Federal spending for financial aid has declined in real dollars by nearly 18%. State aid increased 46.5% in this same period, as did institutional aid (40.9%). The net effect was still a real decline in total aid of 7.6%![20] States attempted to bridge the gap with increased funding for higher education back in the 1980's, but many academic leaders insist that, unless the federal government massively expands financial aid to students, the failure of state governments to sustain past levels of spending on higher education in the 1990's will continue to result in the transfer of responsibility for college costs to students and their parents through higher tuition and fees. Many poor families will not be able to absorb the increase in payments.[21]

Once again, McPherson and Schapiro calculated the average annual change in the level of institutional grants and loans, for the period from 1978 through 1986. The results are displayed in Figure 1.4.[22] Though the biggest increases were for private colleges and universities, the levels of loans increased significantly for all types of institutions.

Family Contributions to Paying for College

Students and their families make their own contributions to paying for college from two primary sources: current earnings at the time of matriculation, and income from savings and investments. The greater the amount a family saves for college, and the greater the return on their investments earmarked for paying for college, the more available to offset the net price of attendance.

Purdue University's Division of Financial Aid conducted a survey in 1989 of the parents of current and prospective students. When asked about savings for college, 49% of the parents of current Purdue students, and 52% of the parents of prospective students indicated that they did not save at all for their children's education.[23] Of those parents who did save, barely one half with children currently attending began saving when their children were in junior high school or before, and only 46% of the parents of prospective students began saving when their children were in junior high school or before.[24]

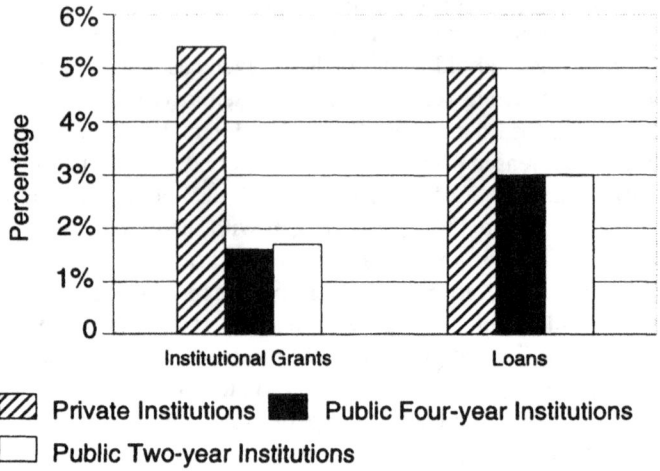

Figure 1.4 - Average Annual Real Change in Aid by Category, 1978 through 1986

Americans do not seem to know how to save, or simply do not choose to do so. Since the early 1970's, personal savings in the United States has dropped significantly as a percentage of GNP, and although business savings as a percentage of GNP has shown an upward trend since the end of World War II, it has declined since the mid-1980's.[25]

Saving is a tricky business. The tax system in the United States provides disincentives for savings especially versus spending on immediate consumption. While earnings spent on consumable goods or services are taxed only once, at the time they are earned, funds saved or invested are usually taxed again when they generate subsequent income. Thus the reward for saving is significantly reduced.[26] Americans, however, have failed to save in the 1980's not so much because of increased consumer spending, but more because their real incomes have not been rising in the eighties and early nineties the way they did in the 1960's and 1970's when the savings rate was closer to 8-10% of after tax income rather than 4-6%.[27]

Saving for college is an even trickier business. Should parents accumulate funds in their names or in their child's? Do increased assets decrease the amount of financial aid for which a student will qualify? Predicting either financial aid availability or financial aid policy into the future is hard enough for financial aid specialists, let alone parents. Other families simply do not know when or how to begin saving, and are more than a little scared about the prospect of affording a $100,000 college education in the year 2000.

Regardless, saving for college is a long term effort, and most parents are small investors who suffer from a variety of problems. Small investors are usually unable to diversify their investments in such a way as to provide protection from changing market conditions. They usually lack both the time and expertise to manage their portfolio properly for this type of long term investment. Lastly, the need to manage long term investments through a number of market cycles is something most small investors cannot clearly see how to do.[28]

Innovations to Increase Family Contribution

Several innovative savings and investments strategies and instruments have appeared in recent years to try to help families increase their contribution to a college education. The College Savings Bank in Princeton, New Jersey has devised and patented savings devices whose rate of return adjusts with the change in the price of tuition at 500 top schools as measured by the College Board. Their current flagship product, the CollegeSure CD, accomplishes this by offering a federally insured instrument. This CD was first offered in 1987. The earnings continue to be taxable, and it is uncertain whether the rate of return can be sustained over the long run.[29]

Meanwhile, the Canadian government has instituted college savings plans with appropriate tax sheltering. The Registered Education Savings Plan is a tax sheltered savings account insured by the Canadian government that earns a high rate of interest. The funds accumulate, and the principal is returned to the parents tax free during the first year that the child attends a post-secondary institution. In subsequent years of matriculation, the earnings are returned directly to the child, and taxed at the child's rate only, often resulting in little or no tax payment at all.[30] By the end of its 1992 fiscal year, the RESP program held over C$300 million in deposits.[31] Legislation proposed by the Bush administration (but not enacted into law by Congress) for a long-term Family Savings Account for education attempted to achieve some of these benefits in the United States as well.[32]

Prepayment Plans as Another Approach

In some ways, the notion of prepayment may mitigate many of the adverse tax effects that interfere with our ability to save. Under this idea, individuals deposit with an intermediary fund that in effect purchases future rights to receive education at the rate of tuition prevailing at the time of the investment. These plans are sometimes set up by individual colleges or universities, sometimes by consortia of colleges and universities or intermediaries, and sometimes by states for their public institutions.

Private consortia have not had much success with prepayment plans. One attempt in the last 1980's was the HEMAR prepayment plan, run by the HEMAR Group of St. Paul, Minnesota.[33] Though it did not get off the ground, this plan claimed to have received several favorable rulings from the Internal Revenue Service and the Securities and Exchange Commission on the status of the investments in the plan. By transferring ownership of the funds to the college or university for which prepayment has been purchased, the accumulated earnings were to be the possession of the educational institution and therefore are not taxable for the student or contributor even upon matriculation.[34] Yet another approach was the creation of a mutual fund by a group of college officials, the College Prepayment Fund, to guarantee that an investor contributing tuition at today's rate would have that tuition apply at the prevailing rate when the student matriculates in the future.[35] This attempt also appears not to have survived into the 1990's, even though representatives of the Fund abandoned their attempts at providing tax sheltering after initiating unsuccessful discussions with the IRS and SEC as far back as 1985.[36]

States have a variety of programs of their own, as displayed in Figure 1.5.[37] While overall the number of states offering tax exempt bond purchase for college tuition use has increased over this period, the number of states offering prepaid tuition plans has remained relatively constant.

State programs have had mixed results. Michigan's program, started in 1986, stopped taking new participants in 1992 based on continued court rulings that, although it is a state program, the funds accumulating in its prepayment trust were still subject to taxation. After

Introduction

the U.S. Court of Appeals ruled in Michigan's favor in November, 1994, the Federal Government decided not to pursue the matter to the Supreme Court.[38] These rulings have cast doubt upon projections made about the viability of the fund.[39]

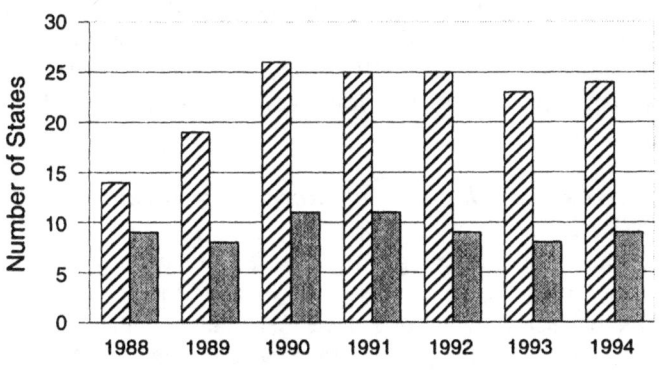

States Offering Tax Exempt Bonds for College Savings
States Offering Prepaid Tuition Plans

Figure 1.5 - State Bond and Prepayment Programs

Pennsylvania, on the other hand, recently enacted both a savings bond program and a college prepayment voucher program. Since each plan was backed by a different part of the state legislature, the governor forged a compromise bill that enacted both measures.[40]

The Critical Issue

Higher education is faced with spiraling costs coupled with great pressure to resist using price increases to balance the budget. Colleges and universities are unable to maintain sufficient revenue to sustain their programs as currently organized. Two solutions are necessary. In the long run, institutions need to find strategies to improve their efficiency and productivity as methods of containing cost. In the short run, institutions need to maximize their revenue and develop better ways of providing price discounts when necessary.

It is this short term issue of revenue maximization that this study is addressing. Banking functions become a strategic necessity for colleges and universities as they face uncertainty over the future of federal and state financial aid, and as families try to maximize their available resources through saving and creative financing. While it is bad enough that many colleges and universities face a relative reduction in revenue in the years to come, and at the same time have trouble curbing their great appetites for spending that developed during the "good years" of the 1980's, many other institutions did not even experience the "good years!"[41] Similarly, many students approach college age without sufficient resources or planning to afford their ultimate goal.

Banking as a Mechanism for Increasing Parental Contribution

Families are struggling to find a safe and structured way to save for college, while at the same time anticipating the need to borrow to meet the balance of their costs once their children matriculate. Their goal is to reduce the net price of attendance through a combination of pre-matriculation savings, tuition payments while their children are in school, and loan repayments after graduation. Colleges and universities control large amounts of cash flowing in and around their organizations and related financial institutions. They have a variety of constituencies able, and perhaps willing, to entrust funds with them for a variety of reasons.

These two big challenges in higher education need to be wedded together. Colleges and universities themselves need to consider becoming financial intermediaries in order to assist their students and families in reducing the net price of attendance. By looking for new sources of capital, and leveraging their ability to coordinate complex financial activities, colleges and universities need to help minimize parental contribution.

Many commercially available programs, such as the HEMAR plan, and the College Prepayment Fund mentioned above, have failed to materialize. Others may provide some good ways for students and their families to save for college, but they may not provide sufficient incentives for some educational institutions to participate. One major problem with commercial plans is the limit in control over and flexibility of the prepayment funds invested. An even more basic problem is the uncertainty over whether the investments themselves will be able to generate sufficient income to make prepayment profitable for the institution. This very problem led to the abandonment of the nation's first prepaid tuition plan by Duquesne University in 1988.[42] The College Savings Bank has evoked similar concern.[43] Other problems concerning the impact on the institution of a plan participant's decision to change institutions are equally unsettling.

Banking functions may provide an option for educational institutions with attributes that current commercial innovations are not prepared to meet. In their simplest form, banks are institutions that (1) take deposits and (2) make loans. They make a profit for their owners or stockholders by charging a higher rate of interest on the money they loan than they pay for savings deposits, and/or by aggregating large sums of money and investing them in preferred instruments. The basic notion of this study is that institutions of higher education can disintermediate banks and bring banking functions in-house just as many commercial enterprises have done (*e.g.*, General Motors with its creation of GMAC), and keep the potential excess revenues for themselves to help reduce the net price of attendance.

Colleges and universities can act as financial intermediaries in one of two ways. First, they can behave as brokerage intermediaries by bringing the buyers and sellers of debt or equity instruments together, for a fee. Second, they can perform what is called portfolio transformation, that is acquire funds through deposits or borrowing and make a profit on investments or loans in a variety of ways. The second of these alternatives is more feasible for higher education institutions. The key issue is to identify the way in which these institutions can make a unique contribution to this brokerage function and therefore capture some profitable portion of the market.[44]

Existing Banking Functions in Colleges and Universities

In many ways, higher education institutions already perform bank-like functions. These functions can generally be divided into three categories. First, the business function of the institution performs bank-like activities through its systems of student billing and receivables, loans and collections. As more institutions experiment with, and implement, tuition prepayment plans they behave even more precisely like banks by aggregating funds received at the beginning of a student's matriculation and investing them until they need to be spent on tuition in subsequent years. While it is true that the majority of student aid loan repayment does not pass through the institution (*i.e.*, Stafford loans), default rates are still tracked by institution.

Second, parts of the institution's operations functions support such services as automated teller machines linked to local banks, short-term loans to some faculty and students, credit unions for students and/or faculty and employees, mortgage programs for faculty and employees, and institution-benefiting credit cards. These enterprises come even closer to being bank-like, and in the case of credit unions the parallels are clearest. Understanding how the educational institution and the related external financial institutions function in each of these instances is important in evaluating the benefits and costs of disintermediating these external institutions.

Finally, the approach with the most potential may be the educational institution's various opportunities as a corporate entity to exploit its significant cash flow and available credit vehicles. As noted above, banks by statute have access to certain preferred sources of funds from the government, and preferred opportunities for investment. Educational institutions themselves, however, have access to unique sources of capital as well, which may be more than sufficient when compared to the costs of being a bank.

Bringing Colleges and Universities Closer to Banking

Many questions need to be answered before a program can be created to try to gain some of these benefits. A more thorough analysis of the differences between various banking institutions needs to be made, with particular emphasis on commercial banks and savings and loans. While banking institutions are heavily regulated, they do enjoy certain tangible benefits over non-banking institutions, especially the availability of funds from the government at extremely favorable rates of interest.

The costs and benefits of being a bank need to be analyzed along several dimensions, including:

(1) *Legal Implications*: It has yet to be determined whether it is legally advantageous or disadvantageous for a college or university to meet the statutory definition of a banking institution. It may be sufficient, or even preferred, that a college or university simply own the banking institution of the type it would like as it would own other entities. Possible implications into the tax exempt status of colleges and

universities, something already under close scrutiny by local, state and federal governments alike, need to also be seriously considered.

(2) *Regulatory Implications*: Colleges and universities are no different than other institutions in wanting as little government regulation as possible, and the constraints, monitors and reporting that usually go along with it. Affirmative action, OMB A-21, OSHA and others are burdensome enough. Since the banking industry is subject to severe government regulation at both the state and federal levels, the potential of such regulation "spilling" into other areas of the academic enterprise that becomes a bank is a serious factor to be considered.

(3) *Political Implications*: Banks wield considerable political influence in government and in society. Their reaction to a new player in the financial community needs to be explored. One could hypothesize a potential outcome of this analysis to be that higher education institutions exert enough influence of their own to be able to get banks to further the goals of the college or university without the need to actually be a bank or even own one.

Outline of the Book

The first part of this book will contain a detailed exploration of the notion of price sensitivity. This key concept is an outgrowth of changes in financial aid on the one hand, and the limits of families' ability to save effectively for college on the other. In Chapter 2, a model will be developed that can be used by an individual college or university to judge the level of price sensitivity being exhibited by students and their families. Three types of institutions will be discussed: highest priced/most selective institutions; other higher-priced/more selective institutions; and lower priced/less selective public institutions. Sample indicators will model conditions of low, moderate and high price sensitivity. In Chapter 3, this model will be tested with actual data from three institutions, one of each type, to assess whether it presents useful measures of price sensitivity.

The second part of the book will focus on banking and intermediation. In Chapter 4, banking functions and structure as they exist in the United States today will be analyzed. After a review of modern banking functions and the structure of the banking industry, a comparison of these different types of banks and "non-bank banks" will be made. In Chapter 5 the "Academic Bank" will be developed as a possible approach that colleges and universities can use to apply banking functions and banking structures to their own student financing problems.

Finally, in Chapter 6, a case study of one institution will be presented to develop an example of the use of banking functions in higher education. This research should provide some viable strategies which could be implemented at this institution or others of similar type. Implications for the other two types of institutions included in the earlier part of the study will also be considered.

Notes

1. "America's Best Colleges: A New Era on Campus," *U.S. News and World Report* (16 October 1989), p. 54.
2. Michael S. McPherson and Morton Owen Schapiro, *Keeping College Affordable: Government and Educational Opportunity* (Washington, D.C.: Brookings Institution, 1991), p. 110.
3. *Ibid.*, p. 117.
4. Based on data from the following sources:

    "The Nation: Resources," *Chronicle of Higher Education Almanac* (5 September 1990), p. 25.

    "The Nation: Resources," *Chronicle of Higher Education Almanac* (28 August 1991), p. 35.

    "The Nation: Resources," *Chronicle of Higher Education Almanac* (26 August 1992), p. 34.

    "The Nation: Resources," *Chronicle of Higher Education Almanac* (25 August 1993), p. 42.

    "The Nation: Resources," *Chronicle of Higher Education Almanac* (1 September 1994), p. 40.
5. William F. Massy, "Productivity Improvement Strategies for College and University Administration and Support Services," Paper Presented at the *Forum for College Financing* (Annapolis: n.p., 26 October 1989), p. 2 and Christopher Shea, "Many Private Colleges Curb Tuition Growth, but Increases Still Outpace Inflation," *Chronicle of Higher Education* (17 March 1993), p. A37.
6. John A. Dunn, Jr., and Dawn G. Terkla, "When is it Going to Stop?: A Speculation on Tuition Rates at One Private University," *Proceedings of the NEAIR 15th Annual Conference* (Providence: Northeast Association for Institutional Research, October 1988), pp. 171-2.
7. Massy, "Productivity Improvement Strategies for College and University Administration and Support Services," pp. 2-8, and William F. Massy, "A Strategy for Productivity Improvement in College and University Academic Departments," Paper Presented at the *Forum for Postsecondary Governance* (Santa Fe: n.p., 30 October 1989), pp. 2-3.
8. Julie L. Nicklin and Goldie Blumenstyk, "Number of Non-Teaching Staff Members Continues to Grow in Higher Education,"

Chronicle of Higher Education (6 January 1993), p. A43.

9. Elaine El-Khawas, "Campus Trends, 1992," *Higher Education Panel Report Number 82* (Washington, D.C.: American Counsel on Education, July 1992), p. 1.

10. *Ibid.*, p. 20.

11. Sonia L. Nazario, "Funding Cuts Take a Toll at University," *Wall Street Journal* (5 October 1992), p. B1.

12. McPherson and Schapiro, p. 110.

13. "Double Trouble," *Policy Perspectives* 2(1) (Philadelphia: University of Pennsylvania, September 1989), p. 5.

14. The full price means what institutions usually refer to as the annual student budget, which includes tuition and fees as well as average room and boards, living, and incidental expenses on a per student basis. Subsequent references to price refer to this amount unless otherwise indicated.

15. As will be discussed below, loans are used in part to discount the full price of attendance. Different methods can be used to calculate the net price taking into account the future payback required on loans used to reduce the full price of attendance.

16. Gwendolyn L. Lewis, "Trends in Student Aid: 1980 to 1988," *Proceedings of the NEAIR 15th Annual Conference* (Providence: Northeast Association for Institutional Research, October 1988), p. 194.

17. Laura Greene Knapp, "Update-Trends in Student Aid: 1981 to 1991" (Washington, D.C.: The College Board, August 1991), p. 10.

18. "Appropriations Bill Would Deny Pell Grants to Some Part-Time Students After January 1," *Chronicle of Higher Education* (18 October 1989), p. A28.

19. "Higher Education's New Majority," *Policy Perspectives* 2(2) (Philadelphia: University of Pennsylvania, January 1990), p. 2.

20. Lawrence E. Gladieux and Gwendolyn L. Lewis, *The Federal Government and Higher Education: Traditions, Trends, Stakes and Issues* (New York: The College Board, 1987), p. 7.

21. Robert L. Jacobson, "Academic Leaders Predict Major Changes for Higher Education in Recession's Wake," *Chronicle of Higher Education* (20 November 1991), p. A35.

22. McPherson and Schapiro, p. 110.

23. Diane Muffett, Marvin Smith and Lee Gordon, "The

Parents' Perspective on Financing Their Child's College Education," Research Report (West Lafayette, IN: Purdue University Division of Financial Aid, 1989), p. 3.

24. Muffett, *et. al*, p. 18.

25. "Save, America: A Primer on U.S. Savings and Its Effect on Economic Health" (Washington, D.C.: Institute for Research on the Economics of Taxation, May 1989), p. 13.

26. Institute for Research on the Economics of Taxation, p. 4.

27. "Personal Savings Rate May Finally Recover," *Wall Street Journal* (2 November 1992), p. A1.

28. Richard E. Anderson, *Tuition Prepayment Guide* (College Park, MD: National Center for Postsecondary Governance and Finance, 1989), pp. 5-6.

29. Michael Quint, "Bank Ties Savings Plan to Rise in College Costs," *New York Times* (21 September 1987), p. D1.

30. "RESP Facts: University Scholarships of Canada Answer Your Questions About Saving for Your Child's Education" (Toronto: University Scholarships of Canada, n.d.), pp. 2-4.

31. *Prospectus: Registered Education Savings Plan* (Toronto: University Scholarships of Canada, 1992), p. 23.

32. "Bush Proposes the Creation of Family Savings Account," *Wall Street Journal* (29 January 1990), p. B2.

33. "National Prepaid-Tuition Program is Started by Company Representing 14 Private Colleges," *Chronicle of Higher Education* (25 October 1989), p. A34.

34. Telephone interview with P. Gregory Stringer (12 January 1990).

35. Joel Dresang, "Pay Now, Learn Later-At Today's Rate," *USA Today* (22 May 1989), p. 3B.

36. Telephone interview with Paul J. McIntyre (15 January 1990).

37. Based on data from the following sources:

"U.S. Roll Call: Tax-Exempt Bonds for College Savings," *Chronicle of Higher Education Almanac* (1 September 1988), p. 12.

"U.S. Roll Call: Prepaid-Tuition Plans," *Chronicle of Higher Education Almanac* (1 September 1988), p. 12.

"9 Issues Affecting Higher Education: a Roll Call of the States," *Chronicle of Higher Education Almanac* (6 September 1989),

p. 10.

"9 Issues Affecting Higher Education: a Roll Call of the States," *Chronicle of Higher Education Almanac* (5 September 1990), p. 8.

"8 Issues Affecting Higher Education: a Roll Call of the States," *Chronicle of Higher Education Almanac* (28 August 1991), p. 10.

"9 Issues Affecting Higher Education: a Roll Call of the States," *Chronicle of Higher Education Almanac* (26 August 1992), p. 8.

"9 Issues Affecting Higher Education: a Roll Call of the States," *Chronicle of Higher Education Almanac* (25 August 1993), p. 10.

"9 Issues Affecting Higher Education: a Roll Call of the States," *Chronicle of Higher Education Almanac* (1 September 1994), p. 12.

38. Patrick Healy, "IRS Abandons Attempt to Tax Michigan's Prepaid-Tuition Plan," *Chronicle of Higher Education* (19 May 1995), p. A33.

39. "State Notes," *Chronicle of Higher Education* (12 August 1992), p. A20.

40. "State Notes," *Chronicle of Higher Education* (15 April 1992), p. A28.

41. "The 1980s: A Financial Retrospective," *Policy Perspectives* 2(1) (Philadelphia: University of Pennsylvania, September 1989), n.p.

42. Gary Putka, "Group of Educators Backs Tuition-Prepayment Plan," *Wall Street Journal* (18 July 1989), p. B1.

43. Richard E. Anderson, "Establishing a Financial Intermediary for College Savings," Unpublished Paper (February 1989), p. 10.

44. *Ibid.*, pp. 5-6.

II
Models of Student Price Sensitivity

Introduction

As colleges and universities struggle with both limits to revenue growth and escalating costs in the 1990's, issues concerning the effect of price on student enrollment decisions will become of major concern to institutional leaders. For over twenty years, the effect of economic factors on student enrollment has been a topic of educational research. These studies were an outgrowth of demand theory, which holds that the demand for a particular good or service (in this case a college education) is a function of several attributes: the price of the good or service, the income or resources of the demander, the price of competing goods and services, and other tastes or preferences that are not price-related.[1]

When it comes to college choice, institutions are growing to believe that price is a major factor in a student's application and matriculation decisions. College is expensive, and many families are not able to afford the full price. Two opposing societal perspectives of who should pay for college exist. On the one hand, it is argued that higher education is a "public good" which benefits everyone and which therefore should be supported with public dollars. On the other hand, it is argued that post-secondary education primarily benefits the recipient and should be paid for by students and their families alone. Both of these perspectives are accepted in the United States, leading to our current mixture of self-payment and government assistance.[2]

Another way to look at these competing views of college financing is to examine them as a struggle between equity and efficiency. An equity argument says that there are private benefits to higher education which will certainly induce those able to afford the price to purchase the product. However, government must intervene to ensure access to higher education for those individuals who are not able to afford it, out of "fairness." An efficiency argument, on the other hand, recognizes that there are private benefits to higher education for individuals, but that there are also public benefits that society at large experiences by having a more educated populace. The greater the degree that government believes these external benefits exist and can be nurtured, the greater the amount of intervention (by encouraging participation through price discounting among other things) it should pursue.[3] Once again, these two notions can be in competition with one another.

These arguments are by and large made at the systemic level. Individual institutions are increasingly recognizing the market forces to which they are subject; prospective students, with incomplete information, are making choices at least in part based on price. The reaction by prospective students to the price set by an institution can create a condition known as price sensitivity. By this it is meant simply that other things being equal, a prospective student will matriculate at the institution that offers the lowest price and ignore other factors such as the academic merits or the overall experience offered by the college or university. In the case of students qualifying for financial aid, price sensitivity favors the institution that offers the best financial aid award. The important distinction here, as discussed in Chapter 1, is that it is the *net* price of attendance that determines what a student will pay out-of-pocket.

If we apply the principles of demand theory to this problem, several possibilities with respect to the effect of price on enrollment (*i.e.* price sensitivity) are likely to be observed. First, we would expect that enrollment rates would go down at a particular institution as the price increases. If there is a surplus of applicants, however, we might see this effect eliminated by the matriculation of other students in the applicant pool who are not price sensitive. Second, we would expect enrollment rates to increase as the quantity and quality of student aid awards get better (since aid functions to effectively reduce net price). Third, we would expect enrollment rates to also increase as the price charged by competing institutions increases.[4]

Leslie and Brinkman have identified no fewer than thirty empirical studies in the area of student demand theory. Their analysis of twenty-five of these studies by and large confirms these observations, though in many cases effects other than the economic ones identified above had a more potent impact on student decisions. Perhaps their most significant observation is that price sensitivity differs based on three major factors: institutional type, price level, and level of student/family income.[5]

While there has been much observed and written in the past

decade about both the cost and price of higher education, there has been no drastic change in participation rates of students. On the other hand, a recent national survey indicates that more students are choosing colleges based on the cost of attendance. While 23% of those students surveyed in 1990 said they had selected their colleges because of low tuition, 27% of those surveyed in 1991 made that indication. Additionally, there was a small increase in the percentage of students who indicated that their financial aid offers had been the determining factor in choosing a college (28% in 1991 up from 25% in 1990).[6] Zemsky and Oedel, writing in the earlier part of the last decade, warned us that one possible outcome of sustained general economic distress is a reduction in the demand for higher education, but more important are increased sensitivity to price and increased price competition especially between different types of higher-priced institutions.[7]

Price sensitivity exists, but to what degree? How can an individual institution understand and measure it for itself? And what can an individual college or university do to counterbalance its effects?

Issues of price sensitivity will now be more fully examined for institutions of three different types: highest-priced/most selective private institutions; other higher-priced/more selective institutions; and lower-priced/less selective public institutions.

Highest-priced/Most Selective Private Institutions: The Overlap Group

Much has been written about the plight of higher-priced institutions, and the many concerns they face. The most elite of these institutions have been very concerned about the effects of price on student enrollment decisions. Twenty-three of these institutions, through several agreements dating back as early as 1958, formed what became known as the Ivy Overlap Group (the explanation of this name will become apparent below) to provide a structure and set of procedures for dealing with these issues.

The guiding principle of the Overlap Group was the notion of need-blind admissions. By this it is meant that the decision to accept or reject a student's application for admission to the institution would not be affected by an assessment of the student's ultimate ability to pay the price of attendance. These institutions also agreed to guarantee that once admitted, sufficient financial assistance would be provided to any student whose family resources were determined to be inadequate to afford the price of attendance. Additionally, the Overlap Group decided that financial aid would be awarded *solely* based on need and not merit.

The Overlap Group was also concerned about the effect of price differences among institutions. It therefore wanted " . . . to neutralize the effect of financial aid so that a student may choose among Ivy Group institutions for *non-financial reasons*."[8] In order to accomplish this, the Overlap Group members met every fall to agree upon a set of guidelines for determining financial need for that year's applicant class. After admission decisions were made and financial aid packaging was determined according to these guidelines and other institutional policies, representatives of the financial aid offices met during the spring to compare the packaging offered to students with overlapping admissions (*i.e.,* those students admitted and awarded aid in more than one Overlap Group institution; thus the name Ivy Overlap). Any differences in need were eliminated (usually to within $500), and at least some attempt was made to equalize packaging as well, namely the mix of outright grant and self-help (loan and work) that a student received. Even after the spring meeting, late awards were compared and adjusted.[9]

This practice persisted until the summer of 1989, when the U.S. Justice Department notified the Overlap Group institutions that an antitrust investigation was beginning. Data were requested from most of the schools in the areas of tuition level, financial aid, and faculty salaries.[10] In the spring of 1991 the Justice Department filed suit in Federal court against the eight institutions in the Overlap Group and MIT, charging them with violating the Sherman Antitrust Act.[11] Specifically, these institutions were charged with colluding to fix the price of higher education through the Ivy Overlap process by eliminating price competition.[12] The government charged that through the activities of the Overlap Group, prospective students were prevented from using price as a basis for their matriculation decisions since the level of their financial aid, which determined their net price of attendance, was equalized across schools. All of the institutions except MIT entered into a consent decree (ultimately affirmed by the U.S. District Court in September, 1991) which specifically restrains them from a set of activities, among them agreeing on any aspect of how need or any component of financial aid policy is determined, exchanging anything but public information on their financial aid policies, tuition levels, or faculty salaries, or discussing any specific awards.[13] Interestingly enough, the consent decree specifically allowed these practices to continue in the context of recruitment of athletes, and allowed outside, independent agencies such as the College Board and its various entities to collect and process financial aid data for these schools.[14]

By refusing to submit, MIT challenged the government's case on several grounds. MIT refuted the government's contention that the Sherman Act even applied. While the government insisted that MIT and the other Overlap Group members were large financial institutions conducting interstate commerce activities due to their recruitment of students from across the country,[15] MIT contended that education could not be considered "interstate commerce," but rather that its activities to provide financial aid were a form of charity that only helped consumers at large and did not hurt them. Even more compelling, MIT argued that contrary to government insistence, any "savings" in financial aid awards due to Ivy Overlap "negotiations" over need and packaging were simply re-applied to some other needy student and never left the area of financial aid to subsidize some other activity of the university.[16]

The outcome of the overlap conferences rarely saved an institution any financial aid funds overall. As an example, whenever the spring meeting determined that an overlap applicant was receiving different levels of self-help, the self-help was always *lowered* to accommodate the student. Whatever institution might have ultimately matriculated the student made up the difference with an additional grant.

In September, 1992 the U.S. District Court for Eastern Pennsylvania rendered its decision in the MIT case. The court ruled against MIT and the Overlap Group. The court did not accept any of MIT's arguments, and did not find the the Sherman Act provides any exception for non-profit institutions of any kind. Stated most succinctly, "the court can conceive of few aspects of higher education that are more commercial than the price charged to students."[17] More striking was the court's rejection of MIT's prediction of the harm that would be caused by the elimination of Overlap. Judge Bechtle wrote,

> The court is unconvinced because there is no evidence supporting MIT's fatalistic prediction that

> the end of the Ivy Overlap Group necessarily would sound the death knell of need-blind admissions or need-based aid.[18]

And later,

> If MIT and the other Ivy League schools were to so easily abandon these objectives merely because Overlap was not in play, then the court could only conclude that their professed dedication to these ends was less than sincere.[19]

The final order prevents any of the schools involved from participating in any collusion to set the price individual students might be charged for attendance.[20]

Was Overlap successful in eliminating price as a determining factor in admissions? While no substantive study was ever done (and is now even less likely due to the terms of the consent decree restricting the exchange of data), evidence seems to suggest that Overlap did eliminate price sensitivity among its members. The government observed in its fact finding that "for nearly 50% of aid applicants who applied to two or more Ivy Group schools, the family contributions each school set before the Spring Meeting varied only slightly."[21] Additionally, the government provides evidence of the effectiveness of Ivy Overlap through its detailing of the attempt in 1986 by the group to get Stanford, a non-participant, to join the group after MIT began to experience significant recruiting losses to Stanford which it attributed to competition in financial aid awards.[22]

It is clear from the participants that Overlap did effectively equalize need and aid packaging and remove price competition between schools. Since the elimination of Overlap, there is evidence that at least some of the participant schools have seen an increased incidence of price competition based on requests by prospective students to review their aid awards specifically because other former Overlap schools have given better packages or determined a higher level of need (the latter is usually the case).[23] This request for review of awards is likely to have the greatest impact on the best Overlap schools, where nearly 90% of the needy admits also apply to other Overlap schools as well. Even less prestigious schools whose needy admitted population is made up of only one third overlap students have seen 35 to 40 cases being requested for appeal per year.

One additional note is required. Part F of the Higher Education Amendments of 1992 to the Higher Education Act of 1965 passed by Congress restores institutions' rights to agree to subscribe to a policy of only need-based financial aid, and agree on general principles for determining need. They may still not, however, discuss the aid packaging for any particular applicant they have in common.

Other Higher-priced/More Selective Institutions

While the activities of the Overlap Group institutions were effective in eliminating price sensitivity when overlap was in practice, many higher-priced institutions were not members of the Overlap Group and did not have those mechanisms to try to reduce price sensitivity. Even among Overlap Group institutions, the overlap process at best eliminated price as a factor among the member schools, not between member schools and other schools.

By and large, these other higher-priced/more selective institutions outside of the Overlap Group also follow a policy of need-blind admissions, and assure applicants that they will provide sufficient financial aid to meet the determined need. There is some evidence, however, that fewer and fewer of these institutions will continue with this policy.[24] Through the 1980's, the surge of need-based financial aid more than likely protected their most needy applicants from price sensitivity by providing sufficient aid. Many of these institutions are small in size and endowment. This makes them particularly sensitive to prospective students leaving these relatively high-priced institutions and matriculating instead at lower-priced/less selective public institutions. These non-Overlap Group institutions will be of particular interest in the coming analysis.

These higher-priced/more selective colleges and universities are best identified by their membership in the Consortium for Financing Higher Education, or COFHE. COFHE studies issues surrounding the financing of higher education among its members, but does not promote the exchange of prospective student data as the Overlap Group did. There are approximately thirty member institutions in COFHE (including, of course, all nine institutions that were parties in the Ivy

Overlap Group complaint), and they tend to be the leading higher-priced, more selective institutions in the United States.

Has the price of these COFHE institutions caused a shift towards lower-priced colleges and universities by price-sensitive students? McPherson and Schapiro have compiled several studies on this issue, and identified a phenomenon they call "middle class melt" to describe the drop in the proportion of American freshman from middle income families attending college. Figure 2.1 shows the change in proportion of all US families with college age children (parents between ages 45 and 64) in three broad income levels compared to the changes in the proportion of all freshman attending college and all freshman attending COFHE colleges in these same three income levels.

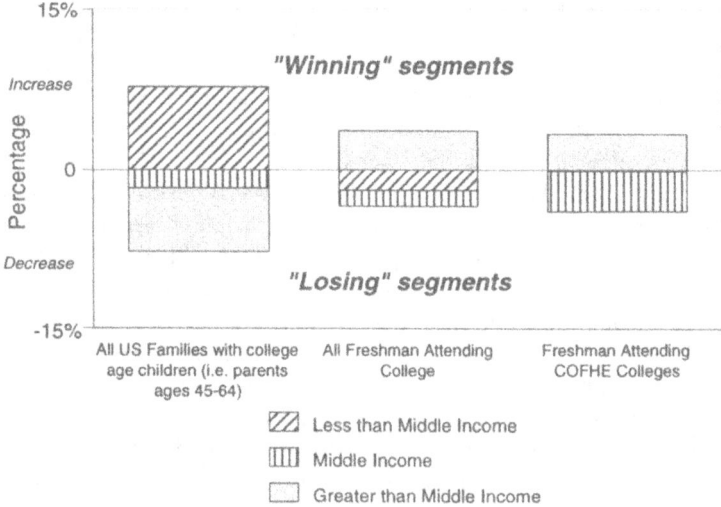

Figure 2.1 - Graph of Percentage Change in Proportions Within Three Broad Income Groups, 1978 to 1989

Interestingly, the data show that while the proportion of lower income families with college age children overall has increased, the proportion of higher than middle income families matriculating at colleges, and at COFHE colleges in particular, has also increased.[25]

Models of Student Price Sensitivity

These data do not confirm the migration of middle income or lower than middle income students to lower-priced institutions. Rather, all institutions are seeing a higher proportion of higher income students attending. We can look further at the phenomenon in COFHE institutions by examining data about the choices of high-performing high school students from middle income families, in this case a sample of students taking the PSAT test who applied for admission to at least one COFHE institution.[26]

	Lower Than Middle Income	Middle Income	Higher Than Middle Income
Applicant Rate	36%	39%	58%
Admit Rate	65%	63%	69%
Matric Rate (Yield)	73%	63%	74%

Table 2.1 - Statistics on High-PSAT COFHE Students, 1987

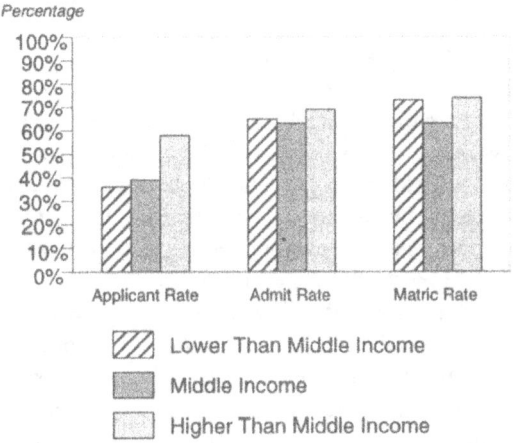

Figure 2.2 - Graph of Statistics on High-PSAT COFHE Students, 1987

Table 2.1 and corresponding Figure 2.2 show a significant difference in application, admission and matriculation based on broad income level. Lower than middle income students applied at a substantially lower rate to COFHE institutions than higher than middle income students. They had a slightly lower chance of being admitted, and a slightly lower chance of actually matriculating. Middle income students faired even worse when it came to admission and matriculation rates. Higher than middle income students faired the best of all.

These data suggest that lower than middle income and middle income students self-selected out of COFHE schools by not even applying (19% difference). The rate of admission for all families was close (all within 6%). This suggests that the admissions staff was indeed practicing need blind admissions in 1987. Most interesting was the difference in matriculation rate for middle income students (approximately 10% lower than both lower than middle income and higher than middle income students).

Were these students price sensitive? Was the published price of attendance a barrier to application for students from middle income families? Is financial aid lowering the price of attendance sufficiently for lower than middle income students, but not sufficiently for middle income students who qualify for less need-based aid? Are middle income students matriculating at lower (net) priced institutions instead?

Lower-priced/Less Selective Public Institutions

Lower priced institutions tend to be public institutions. These colleges and universities generally have substantially lower price tags, not necessarily because they deliver a substantially different product to their students, but rather because the large state subsidy serves the function of lowering tuition not only for the needy but for everyone.[27] Students who matriculate at lower priced institutions tend to have lower family incomes. How sensitive are they to price?

Studies have shown that lower income students especially are sensitive to changes in the price of attendance, that they are less likely to attend an institution as the net price they are expected to pay increases. This sensitivity to price is much less likely among upper income students, and somewhat inconsistent for middle income students.[28] When Tierney looked at the effect of tuition and financial aid on Pennsylvania students who applied to at least one public and one private institution, he found that a student's selection was based primarily on differences in tuition, financial aid, and overall selectivity. He was able to show that the probability of a student matriculating at a private institution decreased as the difference between the tuition of the private and the public institution increased. However, the probability of a student matriculating at a private institution increased as the prestige of the institution increased.[29]

Demand theory tells us that students applying to lower-priced/less selective public institutions should exhibit the greatest price sensitivity. First, for every nominal dollar increase in the price, the increase will be proportionally more at a lower priced college or university. Second, less selective institutions tend to attract lower income students who are known to be more sensitive to price than higher income students. Third, less selective institutions are less likely to have adequate supplemental applicant pools from which to select students in the event that the primary applicant pool reacts negatively to its price.[30]

What steps can a lower priced/less selective college or university take to determine just how sensitive to price its students are? What are the relevant metrics? Are there really differences in the price sensitivity of students applying to these institutions versus higher priced/more selective ones?

A Guide for Institutional Assessment

Price sensitivity exists at different amounts depending on the income levels of the students, and the selectivity of the college or university. Several hypotheses about the sensitivity to price of students applying to three types of institutions—highest-priced/most selective institutions (The "Overlap Group"), other higher-priced/more selective institutions, and lower-priced/less selective public institutions—have been offered. A framework needs to be developed that will allow an *individual* institution to examine its own patterns of pricing, discounting, and enrollment to determine to what degree price sensitivity exists, whether it is changing over time, and what effect price sensitivity may have on student matriculation decisions.

The following section suggests a framework for identifying and analyzing the extent of price sensitivity at an institution. The goal is to present templates that show a given institution how a set of data might appear under conditions of little price sensitivity, moderate price sensitivity, and extreme price sensitivity. Level of price sensitivity falls along a continuum. It is important to identify guideposts near either end of the continuum, and towards the center. The models developed are limited to full-time traditional student enrollment (roughly ages eighteen to twenty-five). While increasing numbers of college-bound students are older than this traditional group, a substantial number of colleges and universities (including the three included in this study) find the vast majority of their students to be traditionally-aged, full-time undergraduates.

A distinction has already been made between the published, full price of attending a college or university ("sticker price"), and lower discounted prices for which some matriculants may be eligible. The net price of attendance is the price the student actually pays, whether it is discounted or not. Need-based, and to a lesser extent, merit-based financial aid represent the largest discounts to price. A study of price sensitivity must focus on the both the full-paying students as well as the students who receive these discounts, and try to determine if there are significant differences between them at an institution.

One method that can be employed to help determine whether price sensitivity exists is to examine differences in characteristics and attributes between the pool of students admitted to an institution, and the subset of this pool that ultimately matriculate at the institution. Students in this first, larger set are admitted to the college or university often without concern about ability to pay (need blind admissions). The basic principle is as follows: if there were *no* price sensitivity, it would be possible to predict certain characteristics of the pool of matriculants based on the pool of admits. To the extent there are differences, price sensitivity is a candidate cause.

The characteristics identified and explored are practical ones, selected both because they may be meaningful measures of the effect of price sensitivity and because they are standard measures used to describe student choice and student pricing in higher education. Since the goal of this analysis is to create a set of templates to be used by any institution, the data selected must be both readily available and easily understood. Three areas of difference between admitted and matriculating students will be examined: differences in yield, differences in total aid for those aided students, and differences in the self-help component of their financial aid packages.

One other aspect of this analysis is important, namely whether any price sensitivity observed at an institution has been stable over a period of time, more evident, or less evident. The models that follow will show a five-year time horizon, and this period represents a reasonable goal for data collection for an institution interested in conducting this analysis for itself.

The First Step: Differences in Yield

Virtually all colleges and universities with competitive admissions (*i.e.*, other than state or local institutions with guaranteed admissions to all state or local residents) track the ratio of the number of matriculating students to the number that were originally admitted to the institution, commonly referred to as the *yield*. While many reasons explain why a student does or does not matriculate at a particular institution, patterns of matriculation may offer clues as to whether price matters.

The first step will be to examine differences in yield, or matriculation rate, for four different groups of students:

> *Needy and aided*: those students who were determined to have financial need, and were awarded at least some need-based aid.
> *Needy and unaided*: those students who were determined to have financial need, but the institution was not able to afford any need-based aid for them.
> *Applied for aid and unaided*: those students who applied for need-based aid, but were determined not to have any legitimate need (and therefore received no need-based aid).
> *Unaided*: those students who neither applied for nor received any need-based aid.

In a college or university exhibiting little or no price sensitivity we would expect little difference in the yield among these categories of students (Figure 2.3, left panel). Students would be just as likely to matriculate at the institution whether they were receiving a price discount or not. As price sensitivity effect begins to take effect, the differences in yield become apparent (center panel) and then even more pronounced (right panel). We would expect students who were needy and unaided, and who applied and were unaided to matriculate at a lower rate than unaided students. We would expect aided students to increasingly matriculate at a higher rate than all the others.

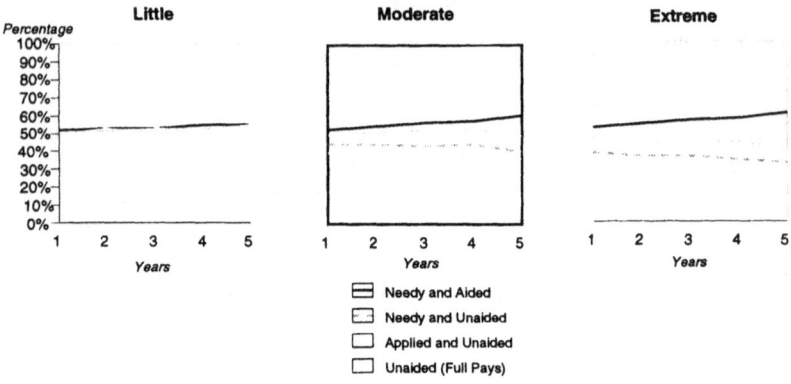

Figure 2.3 - Differences in Yield Percentage

It is possible that the aid awards being offered by the institution are in fact not competitive (*i.e.* "correct") for the market within which the college or university is competing for students. In this case, the matriculation rate (yield) of needy students could *decline* relative to the yield of full-paying students (see additions in Figure 2.4). Worse, if some of the aid awards were competitive and some were not, the effect could become completely muddled and average somewhere in the middle. Under these circumstances there might little apparent difference between the yield of needy and full-paying students.

One way to resolve this dilemma is to identify *two* possible effects on an institution's yield based on price. One, which can be identified as *positive* price sensitivity, occurs when an institution offers competitive financial aid and finds that needy students are matriculating at a *higher* rate than they were admitted. The other, which can be identified as *negative* price sensitivity, occurs when an institution offers non-competitive financial aid and finds that needy students are matriculating at a *lower* rate than they were admitted. As noted above, these two effects can occur simultaneously at the same institution.

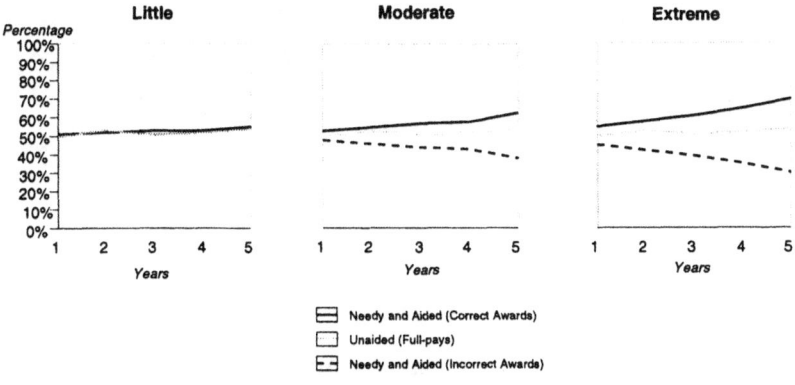

Figure 2.4 - Differences in Yield Percentage Between Needy Admits with Correct Awards, Needy Admits with Incorrect Awards, and Full-paying Admits

To apply this to the three institution types under analysis, it would be expected that Overlap Group awards would be competitive for participating schools during the years that Overlap was in effect at minimum, and likely for several years at least after Overlap was eliminated. Other higher-priced/more selective institutions, on the other hand, may offer the same students vastly different need-based aid awards since they did not benefit from the uniformity that Overlap ensured. Lower-priced/less selective public institutions have significantly lower prices, and often do not practice need-blind admission. Any need-based aid that they do offer is likely to be competitive for institutions of their caliber.

38 The American University and its Banking Function

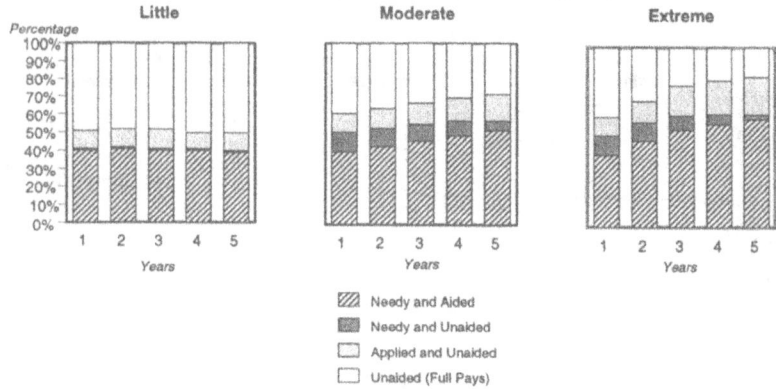

Figure 2.5a - Proportion of Population of Admits by Student Category

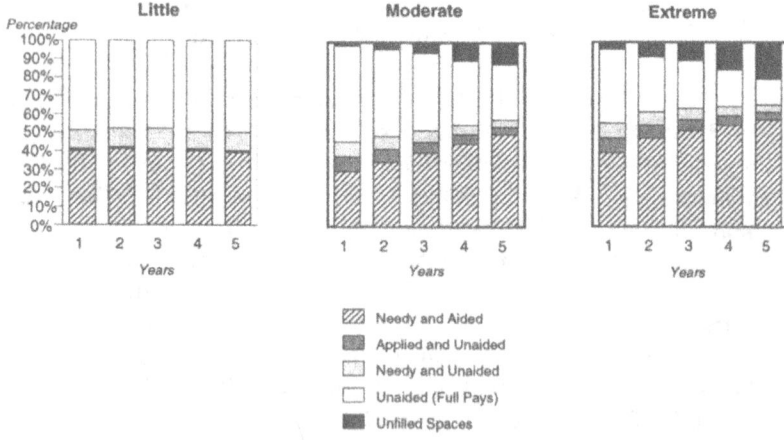

Figure 2.5b - Proportion of Population of Matrics by Student Category

Once differences in yield by the various need and aid categories is examined, the next indicator of price sensitivity is the proportion of students who fall into the various student aid categories (needy and aided, needy and unaided, applied and unaided, unaided). Differences in the proportions within the pool of admitted students, as well as differences within the pool of matriculating students would be expected depending on how sensitive these students were to price (see Figure 2.5a and 2.5b). For the admits, as price sensitivity increases we would expect the proportion of unaided (full pay) students to decrease and the proportion of aided students to increase as aid is increasingly required to attract students. The proportion of applied and unaided students should increase due to additional pressure from non-needy students for financial assistance they feel they deserve (remember, these students in fact do not qualify for need-based aid).

In the pool of matrics, we would expect the proportion of unaided (full pay) students to similarly decrease and the proportion of aided students to increase as aid is increasingly required to attract students. However, the proportion of both those students who applied and were unaided as well as those who were needy but unaided should decline as these price sensitive applicants do not choose to attend the institution. Additionally, we might expect some seats in the incoming class to actually go unfilled if sufficient financial aid is not available to reduce the price of attendance.

Differences Between Admits and Matrics

When focusing on need-based aid, a more detailed analysis is necessary for understanding differences in matriculation rate for different kinds of students. One strategy is to order the aided population of admitted students by total aid, low to high, segment the population (into quintiles, for instance), and to compare and contrast attributes of segments of the population of admitted students with the subset of each segment that matriculates at the institution. Differences that arise between the aid profiles of the admitted and corresponding matriculating students may be attributable to price sensitivity. This notion, and the methods for examining these differences, form the basis for the majority of the analysis which follows. This section will focus on price sensitivity by walking through a series of hypothetical diagrams aimed at displaying how an institution would detect and measure this effect.[31]

To continue the discussion of institutional yield, differences in matriculation would be expected based on the level of aid awarded to a student.

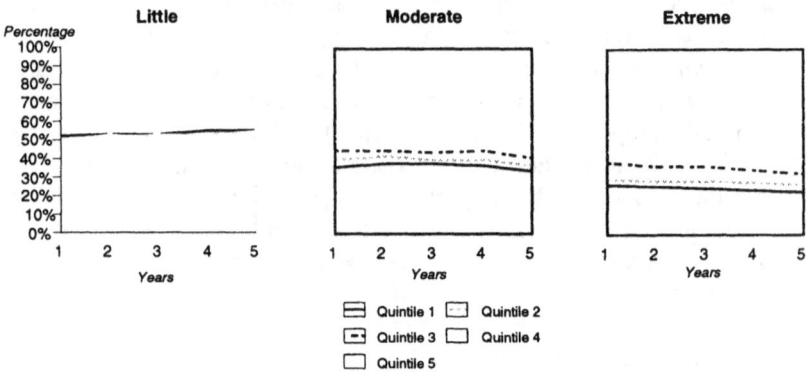

Figure 2.6 - Yield by Quintile of Aid

As price sensitivity increases (see Figure 2.6), the matriculation of students becomes increasingly stratified based on level of aid, with the yield being *highest* for the applicants receiving the most aid (Quintile 1 refers to the *lowest* 20% of aided admits, etc.).

To continue the focus on aided students, in an institution exhibiting price sensitivity the average aid for the matriculants in a segment of the population would be higher than the average aid for that segment of the admits. This shows that a more highly aided subset of matrics is choosing to actually attend this institution than was admitted. The net price these applicants were offered likely has an effect on their decisions. In addition, this trend would continue and increase over time as the effects of price sensitivity worsened.

A comprehensive way to display this effect is to plot the *difference* between the aid of admits and matrics across the various segments of the population.

Models of Student Price Sensitivity 41

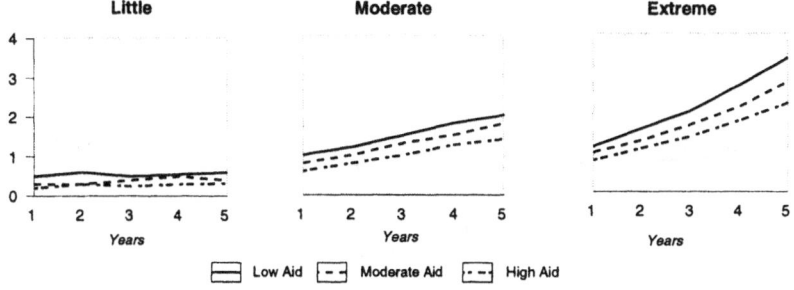

Figure 2.7 - Difference in Aid Between Admits and Matrics
Across the Population
(measured in thousands of dollars)

This difference between admits and matrics is less severe where little price sensitivity is evident (left panel in Figure 2.7), and increasingly more severe as price sensitivity becomes extreme (center, then right panel). Students in lower income brackets should exhibit the most price sensitivity. That is, differences in aid between admits and matrics should be more severe for high aid (meaning lower income) students. However, since the aid awards of high-aid students are likely to be large and sufficiently similar at competing institutions, those students with *low* overall aid will likely exhibit the *most* difference from admits to matrics.

An institution, therefore, can tell much about the sensitivity of its students to price by examining differences in yield, differences in the proportion of the admitted and matriculating populations that fall into various need/aid categories, and differences in aid between admitted and matriculating students. As an additional metric of the difference in aid, it should be interesting to take a look at the level of aid of the admitted population *as a percentage* of the level of aid of the subset matriculating population. This ratio represents another measure of the difference between admits and matrics: the smaller the ratio, the closer the admit and matric populations are to one another in aid, and the less the price sensitivity. The greater the ratio, the greater the difference between admits and matrics and the greater the price sensitivity.

42   The American University and its Banking Function

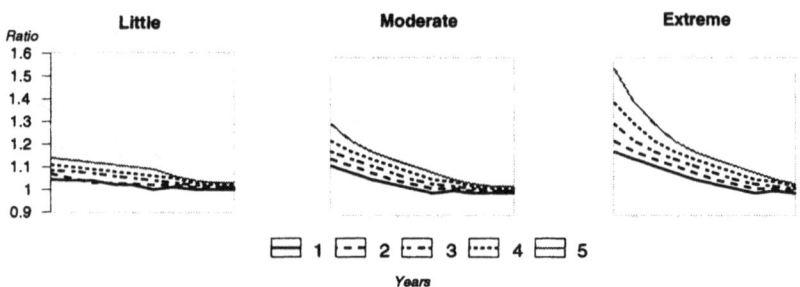

Figure 2.8 - Ratio of Total Aid, Admits to Matrics

Several effects are noticeable (Figure 2.8). First, if the effects of price sensitivity continue over time, that the ratio of aid would be represented by a shifting up of the curve each year that the effect worsens. Second, as the institution moves from conditions of little price sensitivity (left panel) to more extreme price sensitivity (right panel) we would expect all the curves to be shifted up together as the ratio of aid between admits and matrics gets larger as the difference between them increases. Third, as on the previous graph, the effect should be most severe among the low aid students than the high aid students.

     How should an institution understand these expected differences based on aid level? One important factor is the nature of the financial aid packages offered to students, and the differences that may be seen based on overall aid level. The primary measure of the attractiveness of a financial aid award is the proportion of the award that is self help (or conversely the proportion that is grant). By examining the difference in the proportion of the awards by need level that is self help, on average, the institution is one step closer to understanding the price sensitivity.

     Figure 2.9 examines the difference in self help between the population of admits and matrics.

Models of Student Price Sensitivity 43

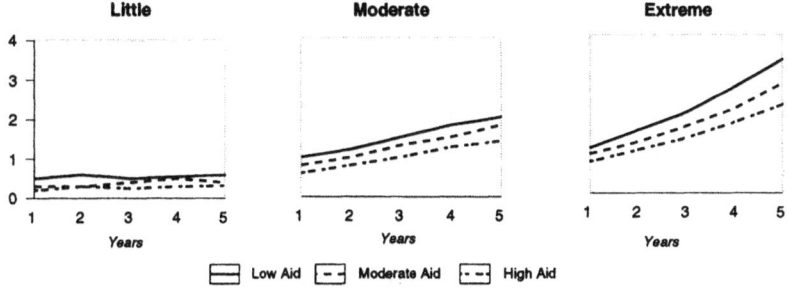

Figure 2.9 - Difference in Amount of Self Help Between
Admits and Matrics
(measured in thousands of dollars)

As with the difference in total aid above, the difference in self help between admits and matrics is less severe where little price sensitivity is evident (left panel in Figure 2.9), and increasingly severe as price sensitivity becomes extreme (center, then right panel).

Similarly, it should be interesting to take a look at the level of self help of the admitted population *as a percentage* of the level of self help of the matriculating population (Figure 2.10). This ratio represents another measure of the difference between admits and matrics: the smaller the ratio, the closer the admit and matric populations are to one another in need, and the less the price sensitivity. The greater the ratio, the greater the difference between admits and matrics and the greater the price sensitivity.

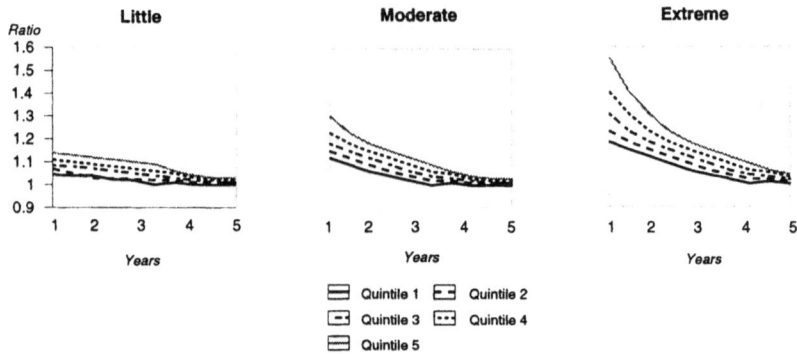

Figure 2.10 - Ratio of Amount of Self Help, Admits to Matrics

In these panels as well the similar downward sloping lines indicate the severity of the effect at the lower end of need, and the lessening severity as need increases. The nesting of the lines indicates the increasing severity due to the increase in price sensitivity over time. Once again, the lines shift downward as the institution moves from a situation of little price sensitivity to one of more extreme price sensitivity.

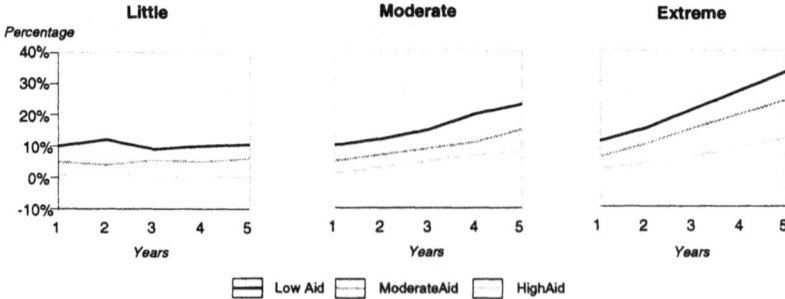

Figure 2.11 - Difference Between Admits and Matrics in the Proportion of Total Aid Award that is Self Help

In an institution exhibiting such price sensitivity, the *difference* in the proportion of self help in aid award packages between the admitted and matriculating populations should become *greater* as price sensitivity becomes more severe. Matriculating students should have *better* aid packages, that is, a *lower* proportion of self help than the larger pool of admits from which they came. This is displayed in the panels in Figure 2.11 by the gradual shifting up of the lines as one moves from the left panel to the center panel and finally to the right panel. An increasing effect over time is evidenced by the changing slope of the lines as one moves from left to right. The most difference in packaging should be evidenced by low aid awards rather than high aid awards.

Implications for an Institution in Aggregate

While differences in aid or self help between the admitted population of students and the subset of this population that ultimately matriculates may seem small, in aggregate these differences may have a significant impact on the ability of the institution to plan its need-based aid awards and deliver them properly. Awards are usually made to the admitted population based on a pool of available dollars for the given aid year. These dollars are a combination of federal, state, and institutional funds. Some are awarded directly by the government to the individual student (like Pell awards), while other are awarded in block grants to the institution as a whole to divide up as it sees fit among eligible students (like SEOG and Work/Study).

An institution assesses its ability to make awards to students at different levels of need based on *average* awards that are calculated for the institution. Since projections of affordability of aid for the entire institution are made based on these average awards, significant differences in the awards of students who actually do matriculate can affect the overall viability of the aid program. To put it more simply, if students are exhibiting price sensitivity, more "aid-expensive" students will matriculate at an institution leaving a potential financial aid shortfall at the aggregate, institutional level.

			Year1 New Student	Year2 New Student	Year3 New Student	Year4 New Student	Year5 New Student
Individual Student	Cost of Attendance	Tuition & Fees	$15,894	$16,848	$17,825	$18,894	$20,028
		Other	$7,786	$8,253	$8,732	$9,256	$9,811
	Parent Contribution		$5,540	$5,706	$5,992	$6,171	$6,356
	Student Contribution		$1,758	$1,811	$1,901	$1,958	$2,017
	Pell, State and Other Grants		$1,394	$1,326	$1,296	$1,329	$1,329
	SEOG		$738	$696	$675	$696	$696
	Endowment		$417	$649	$692	$785	$864
	Planned Unmet Need		$140	$132	$128	$132	$132
	Need		$13,693	$14,781	$15,872	$17,079	$18,446
	Self Help	Perkins Loan	$936	$983	$1,032	$1,084	$1,138
		Stafford Loan	$2,198	$2,308	$2,423	$2,544	$2,625
		Institutional Loan	$167	$175	$184	$193	$203
		Work/Study	$1,346	$1,413	$1,484	$1,558	$1,636
		Total	$4,647	$4,879	$5,123	$5,379	$5,602
	Unrestricted Budget Need		$9,046	$9,901	$10,749	$11,700	$12,844

Table 2.2 - Aid Estimate for a Single Student

Table 2.2 displays a typical financial aid estimate for a single first year student at a high-priced institution over five years. The institution is using "real" values for the first year, then estimating the impact on future years based on a set of growth factors. In this case the institution was focusing its analysis on the expected change in demand for its institutional grant funds (labeled "Unrestricted Budget Need" in this table). These funds are needed to bridge the gap between available external financial aid (federal and state provided as well as private funds) and need. Note in this model the growing need for institutional grant funds on average ranging from just over $9,000 per student in the first year to almost $13,000 per student in the fifth year.

			Year1 New Students	Year2 New Students	Year3 New Students	Year4 New Students	Year5 New Students
Institution	Cost of Attendance	Tuition & Fees	$13,748,310	$14,573,209	$15,418,455	$16,343,562	$17,324,176
		Other	$6,734,890	$7,138,983	$7,553,044	$8,006,227	$8,486,601
	Parent Contribution		$4,792,100	$4,935,863	$5,182,656	$5,338,136	$5,498,280
	Student Contribution		$1,520,670	$1,566,290	$1,644,605	$1,693,943	$1,744,761
	Pell, State and Other Grants		$1,205,810	$1,147,213	$1,121,302	$1,149,349	$1,149,349
	SEOG		$638,376	$602,022	$583,750	$601,703	$601,703
	Endowment		$360,882	$561,545	$598,951	$679,108	$747,019
	Planned Unmet Need		$120,997	$114,107	$110,643	$114,046	$114,046
	Need		$11,844,365	$12,785,152	$13,729,592	$14,773,504	$15,955,618
	Self Help	Perkins Loan	$809,640	$850,122	$892,628	$937,260	$984,122
		Stafford Loan	$1,901,270	$1,996,334	$2,096,150	$2,200,958	$2,270,625
		Institutional Loan	$144,455	$151,678	$159,262	$167,225	$175,586
		Work/Study	$1,164,290	$1,222,505	$1,283,630	$1,347,811	$1,415,202
		Total	$4,019,655	$4,220,638	$4,431,670	$4,653,253	$4,845,535
	Unrestricted Budget Need		$7,824,710	$8,564,515	$9,297,922	$10,120,251	$11,110,083

Table 2.3 - Aid Estimate for Entire Entering Class

Table 2.3 displays this same estimate for an entire entering class at the same institution. Any significant deviation from the *average* award modeled in Table 2.3, and carried forward in Table 2.4, can have a significant impact on this institution's ability to deliver the aid it promises. More important, if the institution fails to recognize the possibility that its actual awards may vary significantly from its average projected awards, it can find itself with the total of its awards accepted being larger than the total aid it has available for distribution.

Summary

Table 2.4 summarizes the pieces of the model, the measures of price sensitivity, that has been developed.

		Description
Yield	Differences in Yield Percentages	Comparing yield of Needy and Aided, Needy and Unaided, Applied and Unaided, and Full Pay students.
	Proportion of Population by Student Category	Separately for admits and matrics, comparing yield of Needy and Aided, Needy and Unaided, Applied and Unaided, and Full Pay
	Yield by Quintile of Aid	Comparing yield by quintile of aid.
Total Aid	Difference in Average Total Aid Between Admits and Matrics	Comparing differences in total aid, based on low, moderate, and high aid levels.
	Ratio of Total Aid, Admits to Matrics	Comparing the ratio of total aid across quintiles of aid separately for multiple years.
Self Help	Difference in Amount of Self Help Between Admits and Matrics	Comparing differences in self help, based on low, moderate, and high aid levels.
	Ratio of Amount of Self Help, Admits to Matrics	Comparing the ratio of self help across quintiles of aid separately for multiple years.
	Difference in Proportion of Total Aid that is Self Help	Comparing the proportion of total aid award packages that is self help, based on low, moderate and high aid levels.

Table 2.4 - Institutional Self-assessment of Price Sensitivity

The next chapter applies these concepts to data from three schools of different types to see how well the models of price sensitivity developed here help describe conditions at these three institutions, and how the implications of the model compare with the perceptions of price sensitivity that these institutions hold about themselves.

Notes

1. Larry L. Leslie and Paul T. Brinkman, "Student Price Response in Higher Education: The Student Demand Studies," *Journal of Higher Education* 58(2) (1987), pp. 181-2.
2. Chester E. Finn, Jr., *Scholars, Dollars & Bureaucrats* (Washington, D.C.: The Brookings Institution, 1978), p. 46.
3. David W. Breneman and Susan C. Nelson, *Financing Community Colleges: An Economic Perspective* (Washington, D.C.: Brookings Institution, 1981), pp. 28-30.
4. *Ibid.*, p. 181.
5. *Ibid.*, pp. 198-200.
6. Michele N-K Collison, "More Freshman Say They Are Choosing Colleges Based on Cost," *Chronicle of Higher Education* (22 January 1992), p. A33.
7. Robert Zemsky and Penney Oedel, *The Structure of College Choice* (New York: College Entrance Examination Board, 1983), pp. 88-9.
8. Manual of the Counsel of Ivy Presidents, *Section X: Admissions and Financial Aid*, revised 11/87, p. 30. (emphasis added)
9. *Idem.*, and United States of America v. Brown University et al., 91-CV-3274, "Government's Statement of Principal Factual Issues for Litigation" (20 April 1992), pp. 1-3.
10. Paul M. Barrett, "U.S. Investigates Prestigious Universities, Colleges for Possible Antitrust Violations," *Wall Street Journal* (10 August 1989), p. B2.
11. Sherman Act, 15 U.S.C. sec 1 (1982).
12. United States of America v. Brown University *et al.*, 91-CV-3274, "Government's Motion for Summary Judgement" (3 April 1992), p. 3.
13. United States of America v. Brown University *et al.*, 91-CV-3274, "Final Judgement" (19 September 1991), p. 10.
14. *Ibid.*, pp. 4-5.
15. United States of America v. Brown University *et al.*, "Government's Motion for Summary Judgement," p. 5.
16. United States of America v. Brown University *et al.*, 91-CV-3274, "Massachusetts Institute of Technology's Pretrial Memorandum" (22 May 1992), pp. 2-3.

17. United States of America v. Brown University *et al.*, 91-CV-3274, "Decision and Order" (2 September 1992), p. 26.
18. *Ibid.*, p. 46.
19. *Ibid.*, p. 47.
20. United States of America v. Brown University *et al.*, 91-CV-3274, "Order" (2 September 1992), p. 2.
21. United States of America v. Brown University *et al.*, "Government's Statement of Principal Factual Issues for Litigation," p. 2.
22. United States of America v. Brown University *et al.*, 91-CV-3274, "Memorandum of Law in Support of Government's Motion for Summary Judgement" (3 April 1992), pp 50-4.
23. Scott Calvert, "After Overlap, Financial Aid Changes," *The Summer Pennsylvanian* (23 July 1992), p. 1.
24. Lee Mitgang, "Elite Colleges Pull Back from Guaranteed Student Aid," *Philadelphia Inquirer* (24 December 1991), p. 4-A.
25. McPherson and Schapiro, p. 80.
26. *Ibid.*, p. 92.
27. *Ibid.*, p. 135.
28. *Ibid.*, pp. 53-4.
29. Michael L. Tierney, "The Impact of Financial Aid on Student Demand for Public/Private Higher Education," *Journal of Higher Education* 51(5) (1980), p. 541.
30. Leslie and Brinkman, p. 198.
31. Assume unless specifically noted that all references to price sensitivity for the remainder of the chapter are to positive price sensitivity. Clearly, negative price sensitivity would have an exactly opposite mirror effect on an institution. If both positive and negative price sensitivity were taking place, the observations would likely be completely muddled, and appear as a less severe case of the dominant effect (positive or negative).

III
Student Price Sensitivity: Results from Three Schools

Introduction

In the previous chapter a framework was developed for examining how student price sensitivity might be exhibited in the data of a typical college or university. The models developed showed examples of little, moderate and extreme price sensitivity. This chapter will test how well these models serve as guides against which individual colleges or universities can evaluate the level of price sensitivity using actual data from real institutions. Observing change over time is also a major concern.

In Chapter 2 three different types of institutions were discussed. The first group contained the highest priced/most selective institutions characterized by the Overlap Group. Second were the other higher-priced, more selective institutions typified by the smaller, expensive liberal arts college. Third were the public colleges which fall into the lower priced/less selective institution category.

Actual Results

In order to test the hypotheses discussed in the previous chapter, actual data were collected from three institutions, one representative of each of these three groups. The Carnegie Commission on Higher Education devised a complex system of classification for colleges and universities.[1] Baldridge *et al.* present a simplified eight-category typology.[2] By this framework, one of the institutions is a private multiversity (to be referred to as PMU), the second is a private liberal arts college (to be referred to as PLA). The third is a public comprehensive (to be referred to as PUC). Institutions of different types were chosen to study the possible difference in effect. For PMU, six years worth of data were available, for students who would be matriculating from the fall of 1987 through the fall of 1992. For PLA three years worth of data were available, fall 1987 through fall 1991. For PUC, only two years worth of data were available, fall 1991 and fall 1992.

For PMU, the data for admits represent all those students who were admitted to one of the four full-time undergraduate day programs at the university. Only fall semester admits were included, though all students in the sample were requesting admission for the fall and spring semesters together. Several samples were acquired. The main sample contained all students admitted with a positive "need" calculated for them through the standard Congressional Methodology by the school's Financial Aid Office. Packaging information was also provided. A second sample provided information on those admitted students who applied for financial aid but were not determined to have any need. Aggregate data were also provided on total applicants, admits and matriculants for all the years indicated.

For PLA, the data for admits and matrics were provided for all U.S. student applicants with financial need. Packaging information was not available. It was indicated by the institution that need-based aid was provided to cover all calculated need, so in this instance total need was used as a surrogate for total aid in the analysis.

Integrating PUC data proved a little more challenging. At a public institution, state-resident matriculants and non-resident matriculants face very different prices for attendance. It was necessary to segment the data received from PUC into separate data sets, one for resident students and one for non-resident students. This was done based on the "budget" (or price of attendance) data provided with each data point. Part-time students were eliminated for consistency, as were financially "independent" students. Both sets were identified based on budget for attendance.

Other accommodations needed to be made for PUC data. PMU and PLA considered "need-based aid" to be subsidized federal programs (like Pell, SEOG, NDSL, GSL and Work/Study), state need-based grant programs, and institutional grant and loan programs. Unsubsidized government programs, like Plus and SLS loans for students and their families, were excluded from this definition. PMU data needed to be adjusted to exclude amounts from these programs from the data, and sufficient information was provided to make this adjustment possible.

One additional clarification is necessary with respect to PUC. Because of the vast difference between resident and non-resident students, they were treated as separate data sets and will be presented

Student Price Sensitivity: Results from Three Schools

below separately. For reasons of comparison, the attributes and behavior of the non-resident students are closer to those of PMU and PLA students, so their data are presented first, with resident student data shown for additional comparison.

The following is an analysis of the actual data received from these three institutions using the models developed in the previous chapter. The goal is to evaluate the effectiveness of these models in identifying whether the three institutions are exhibiting price sensitivity. Emphasis will be placed on the degree of price sensitivity, and how stable or volatile any price sensitivity was over time.

1. Difference in yield

Data were available to some degree from each school on differences in yield between admits and matrics. Tables 3.1 through 3.3 show the values.

	1987	1988	1989	1990	1991	1992
All						
Admit	4,871	4,605	4,580	4,527	4,603	4,948
Matric	2,505	2,268	2,281	2,231	2,315	2,295
Yield	51.43%	49.25%	49.80%	49.28%	50.29%	46.38%
Needy & Aided						
Admit	2,052	1,814	1,842	1,799	1,792	1,852
Matric	1,096	931	954	991	961	942
Yield	53.41%	51.32%	51.79%	55.09%	53.63%	50.86%
Needy & Unaided						
Admit	34	29	21	16	9	34
Matric	30	21	17	10	6	6
Yield	88.24%	72.41%	80.95%	62.50%	66.67%	17.65%
Applied & Unaided						
Admit	551	531	572	554	540	623
Matric	252	232	251	209	237	242
Yield	45.74%	43.69%	43.88%	37.73%	43.89%	38.84%
Unaided						
Admit	2,234	2,231	2,145	2,158	2,262	2,439
Matric	1,127	1,084	1,059	1,021	1,111	1,105
Yield	50.45%	48.59%	49.37%	47.31%	49.12%	45.31%

Table 3.1 - Differences in Yield Percentage, PMU

	1987	1988	1989	1990	1991	1992
All						
Admit			1,677	1,864	1,930	
Matric			460	500	500	
Yield			27.43%	26.82%	25.91%	
Needy & Aided						
Admit			416	657	475	
Matric			105	233	124	
Yield			25.24%	35.46%	26.11%	
Unaided						
Admit			1,261	1,207	1,455	
Matric			355	267	376	
Yield			28.15%	22.12%	25.84%	

Table 3.2 - Differences in Yield Percentage, PLA

	1987	1988	1989	1990	1991	1992
All						
Admit					8,887	8,339
Matric					2,447	2,132
Yield					27.53%	25.57%
Needy & Aided						
Admit					1,413	1,509
Matric					629	545
Yield					44.52%	36.12%
Needy & Unaided						
Admit					744	768
Matric					75	111
Yield					10.08%	14.45%
Unaided						
Admit					6,730	6,062
Matric					1,743	1,476
Yield					25.90%	24.35%

Table 3.3a - Differences in Yield Percentage, PUC Non-residents

	1987	1988	1989	1990	1991	1992
All						
Admit					1,308	1,414
Matric					818	911
Yield					62.54%	64.43%
Needy & Aided						
Admit					251	329
Matric					205	239
Yield					81.67%	72.64%
Needy & Unaided						
Admit					97	99
Matric					49	34
Yield					50.52%	34.34%
Unaided						
Admit					960	986
Matric					564	638
Yield					58.75%	64.71%

Table 3.3b - Differences in Yield Percentage, PUC Residents

Figure 3.1 presents a graphical display of the differences in yield. For PMU, there is an expected stratification in the yield percentages for an institution exhibiting at least some price sensitivity: the yield for those who were needy and aided is the highest, above the yield for those unaided, which was higher than those who applied for aid and were not determined to be needy.[3] This suggest that student choice to attend was at least somewhat dependent on net price of attendance (or the perception of net price): aided students with the lowest net price matriculated in the highest proportion, and students who felt they deserved aid but did not get it matriculated in the lowest proportion. All the data were relatively consistent across the six years.

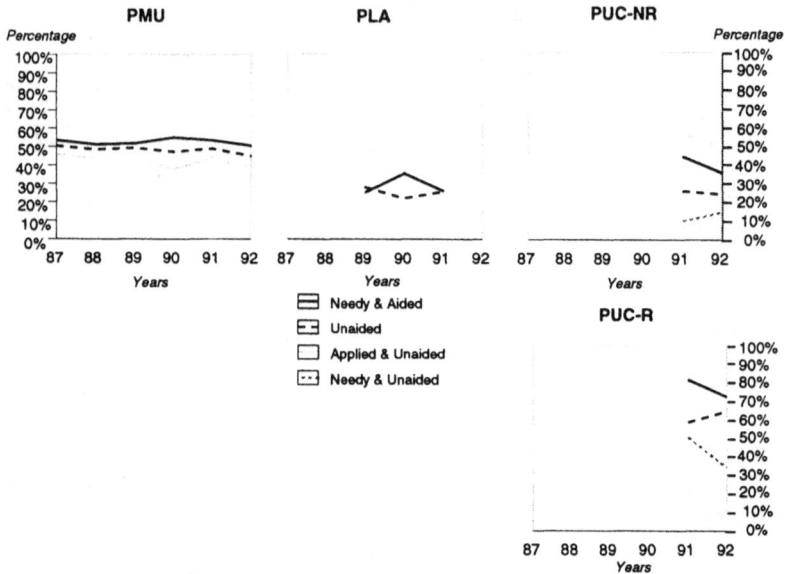

Figure 3.1 - Differences in Yield Percentage[4]

For PLA the situation is slightly different. Aid seemed to have no affect on decision to matriculate in 1989 and 1991, but there seems to be some change in 1990 that has led aided students to matriculate at a noticeably higher rate. This suggests some intervention by the administration at that college in 1990 that caused price to be a factor in the decision.

The pattern for PUC is similar to the pattern for PMU. Needy and aided students matriculated at a higher proportion than unaided students, who matriculated at a higher proportion than needy and unaided students in this case.[5] The stratification holds true for both non-state-resident and state-resident students. For non-resident students, there seems to be a slight trend toward less price sensitivity, with the yield rates between aided and needy and unaided students narrowing significantly. For resident students, the results are hard to interpret. The yield for both aided students and needy and unaided students went down from 1991 to 1992, while the yield for unaided

Student Price Sensitivity: Results from Three Schools

students increased!

Figure 3.2 shows the proportion of each type of applicant and matriculant that is represented in each population.

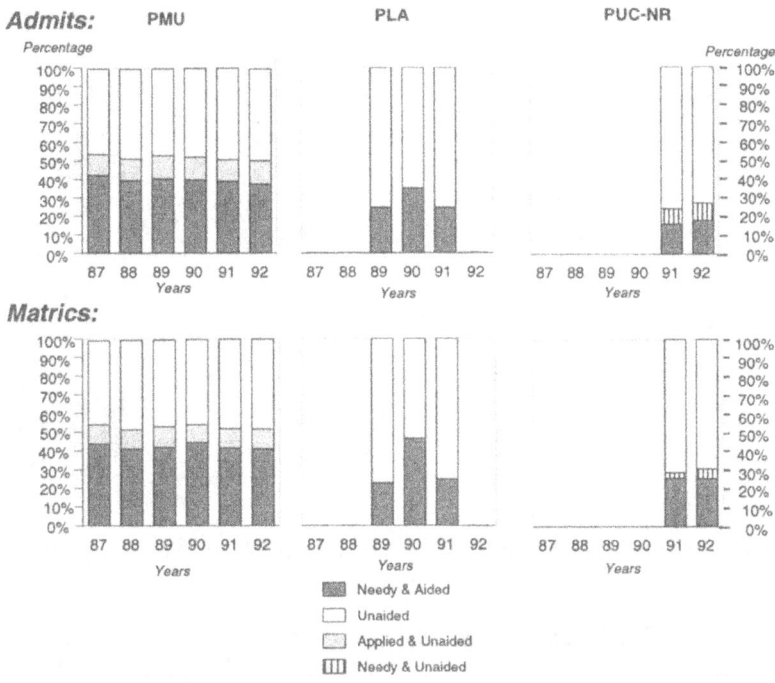

Figure 3.2a - Proportion of Population by Student Category

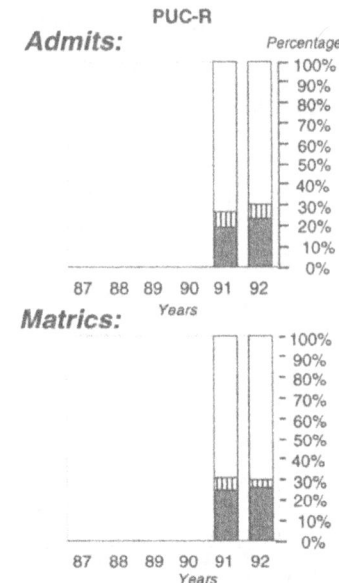

Figure 3.2b - Proportion of Population by Student Category (continued)

For PMU, there was virtually no difference in the proportion of admits or matrics who were needy and aided, had applied for aid and been unaided, or who had not applied and been unaided. There was little difference over time either. For PLA, once again, there is almost no difference between the proportion of aided and unaided students for 1989 and 1991, but a significant difference in 1990. Not only is there a significantly larger proportion of the admits who are awarded aid, but the proportion of matrics who are aided is even more pronounced in 1990. This shows that in 1990 students were *very* sensitive to price: an extremely high proportion of the needy and aided students matriculated, in greater proportion than they had been accepted, likely because of the decrease in net price caused by the need-based aid.

PUC is the only institution with a noticeable number of needy but unaided students. Among the section of the population that is not state resident, there is a similar proportion of aided matriculants in both years. Among the admits, however, there is a noticeably larger proportion of needy and unaided students in both years. Clearly, a smaller proportion of needy and unaided students chose to matriculate than the proportion admitted, indicating some degree of sensitivity to price on the part of these students. A higher proportion of them chose to matriculate in 1992, indicating a possible softening of the effect. For PUC students who were state residents, the data for admits are almost identical. For matrics, however, 1992 saw a smaller rather than a larger proportion of needy and unaided students in the population.

As a college or university examines the proportions of needy, aided and unaided students that are admitted and matriculate, as well as the proportion of unfilled class seats if any, it must be looking for patterns similar to the ones observed above. PMU shows a relatively stable pattern of an institution with admits who matriculate in relative constant proportion whether they receive aid or not. By this measure PMU students are exhibiting little price sensitivity. PLA shows the instability of a college with moderate price sensitivity where in one year aid students matriculate in much higher proportion based on financial aid price discounting. PUC shows some more subtle effects of price sensitivity as students who are needy but unaided choose not to matriculate.

One additional measure of yield is important. If the population of aided students is sorted in order of overall aid, and broken into quintiles, any differences in yield based on aid level could be identified. Figure 3.3 shows the data for the three schools.

PMU is stratified by quintile, indicating moderate price sensitivity by this measure. The greater the aid, the higher the yield rate; the lesser the aid, the lower the yield rate. This trend appears relatively consistent over the six years, with a somewhat lower yield among lesser aided students in 1992.

PLA's data is by and large stratified as well. Once again, yield was significantly increased in 1990 for the upper three quintiles of the population, and this increased yield seems to have persisted into 1991 for the most aided students. Yield for the lesser aided students remained steady or even declined over the three years.

60   The American University and its Banking Function

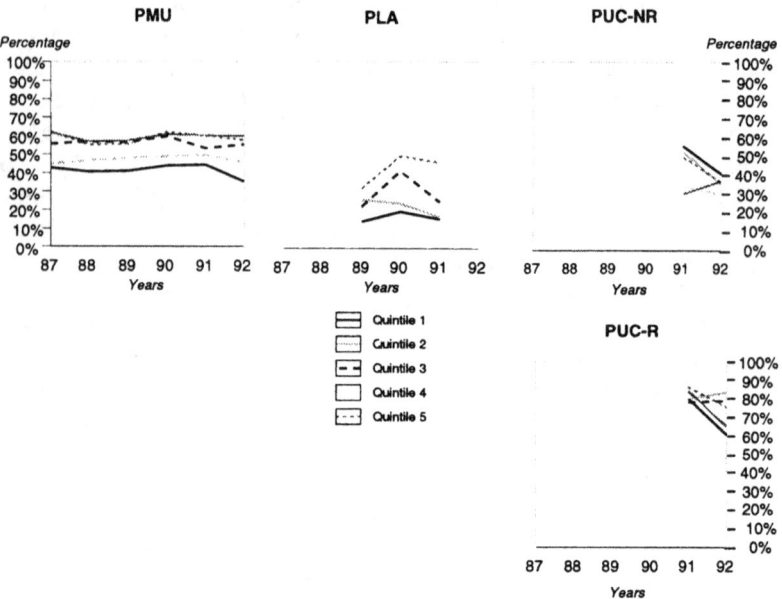

Figure 3.3 - Yield by Quintile of Aid[6]

PUC data shows a very different picture. For the non-state residents, there appears to be no pattern in the yield rates of the quintiles of aided students, but in some cases wide differences. By 1992, these differences disappear, and there is virtually identical yield regardless of aid level. This indicates that while the yield of needy and aided students is higher than unaided students, suggesting some price sensitivity (see Figure 3.1), there is little difference in yield for students with different levels of aid. The resident students at PUC show the same randomness in yield rates by quintile of aid, but here the differences in yield are much *less* pronounced in 1991 than in 1992. The position of the lines along the vertical axis on the graph for PUC resident students indicates a much higher yield rate overall for the aided students.

Student Price Sensitivity: Results from Three Schools

2. Differences in Aid Between Admits and Matrics

The analysis now concentrates on the differences that may exist between admitted and matriculating students who received aid only. There are no additional data on unaided students that might help explain just how sensitive to price these students may be. Financial aid, however, has the effect of reducing the net price of attendance, so examining the effect of different levels of aid on the decision to matriculate may shed light on this phenomenon.

Tables 3.4a through 3.4d show the average total aid for admitted students by quintile of the aided population (that is, the first quintile represents the first 20% of aided students, those receiving the least aid). Also shown is the difference between the average aid of the admits and the subset of each quintile that actually matriculated.

		1987	1988	1989	1990	1991	1992
Admits	1	$3,276	$3,394	$3,960	$4,684	$4,553	$4,800
	2	$7,938	$8,122	$9,053	$10,107	$10,302	$10,918
	3	$11,095	$11,480	$12,545	$13,731	$14,463	$15,454
	4	$13,603	$14,271	$15,452	$16,902	$17,738	$18,946
	5	$16,323	$17,325	$18,612	$20,059	$21,275	$22,523
Difference Between Admits and Matrics (Matrics - Admits)	1	$232	$113	$182	$187	$225	$517
	2	($10)	$72	$146	$94	$175	($50)
	3	$73	$64	$24	($13)	$36	$116
	4	$41	$37	$11	$63	($7)	$29
	5	$42	$37	($35)	$47	$47	($49)

Table 3.4a - Average Total Aid for PMU, by Quintile

		1987	1988	1989	1990	1991	1992
Admits	1			$3,768	$4,050	$3,713	
	2			$6,330	$8,809	$9,245	
	3			$9,795	$12,390	$13,035	
	4			$12,940	$15,327	$16,336	
	5			$16,170	$18,577	$19,582	
Difference Between Admits and Matrics (Matrics - Admits)	1			($689)	$98	$567	
	2			$210	($37)	$632	
	3			$178	$196	$295	
	4			$251	$196	$30	
	5			($282)	$37	($18)	

Table 3.4b - Average Total Need for PLA, by Quintile

		1987	1988	1989	1990	1991	1992
Admits	1					$1,751	$1,887
	2					$3,441	$2,954
	3					$5,036	$4,226
	4					$5,911	$5,546
	5					$9,027	$9,139
Difference Between Admits and Matrics (Matrics - Admits)	1					($40)	($88)
	2					($107)	$39
	3					($84)	$0
	4					$221	$96
	5					$545	$658

Table 3.4c - Average Total Aid for PUC Non-state Residents, by Quintile

		1987	1988	1989	1990	1991	1992
Admits	1					$1,057	$1,598
	2					$2,350	$2,917
	3					$3,615	$4,271
	4					$5,092	$5,592
	5					$7,773	$7,775
Difference Between Admits and Matrics (Matrics - Admits)	1					$2	$5
	2					$2	$15
	3					($34)	$12
	4					($89)	$135
	5					($88)	($130)

Table 3.4d - Average Total Aid for PUC State Residents, by Quintile

Positive numbers in the bottom half of each table indicate that, for those cells, matriculating students on average received better aid awards than admitted students. The more positive the numbers the greater the effect of price on the decision to matriculate; if price was not a factor, the aid level of matriculating students would be no different on average than the aid level for admitted students within each aid range (quintile).

This difference is displayed graphically in Figure 3.4. For PMU, most of the aid quintiles show little difference between admits and matrics. Only the lowest aid quintile shows any noticeable difference, with some peaking in 1992. Keep in mind, however, that the tuition and fee level at this institution was in excess of $10,000 in 1987 and almost $16,000 in 1992. The total price of attendance (tuition and fees plus room and board and living expenses) was significantly above that. Even the greatest difference in total aid represents at most just over 3% of the level of tuition, and no more than 2% of the overall budget.

Student Price Sensitivity: Results from Three Schools 63

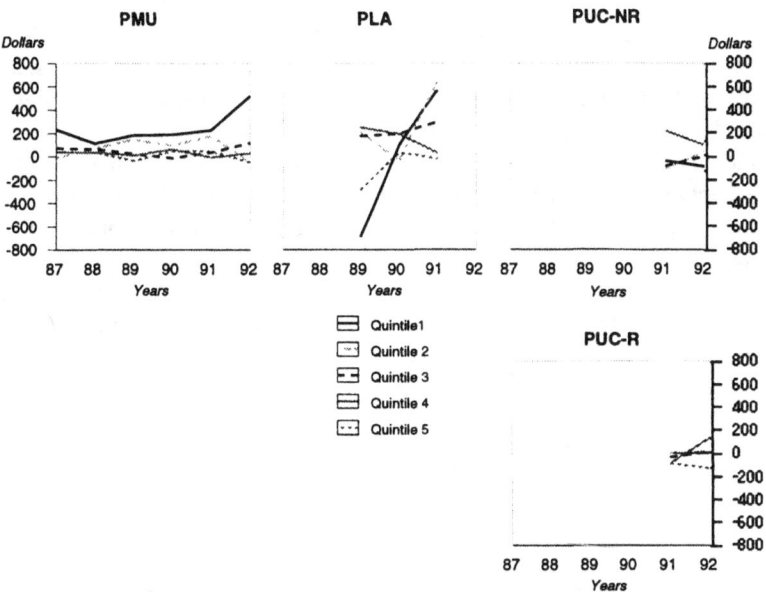

Figure 3.4 - Difference in Average Total Aid Between Admits and Matrics

For PLA the data are more erratic. For the lowest need/aid quintile, matrics start out in 1989 with actually lower aid levels than admits. This means that the institution was not able to use price discounts to effectively recruit students. To a lesser degree the same appears to be true for the highest need/aid quintile. By 1990 there was little difference at all in either quintile (1 or 5), but by 1991 the pendulum had swung the other way for the lowest need/aid quintile. Those students who were matriculating all of a sudden had higher aid awards than those admitted. For the remaining deciles, matriculating students maintained an edge, and this edge increased as time went on for deciles 2 and 3. These results show the erratic nature of the market for students within which liberal arts colleges such as PLA compete.

For PUC the results are somewhat different. First for non-state residents, in the low aid quintiles 1, 2 and 3 there is little difference in aid between admits and matrics in 1991, and virtually no difference by 1992. The higher aid quintiles show a much greater difference favoring the matrics, with the effect easing somewhat for quintile 4 by 1992 and becoming greater for quintile 5 by 1992. This difference in 1992 accounts for nearly 5% of the overall budget for attendance. For state residents, there is nearly no difference in total aid between admitted students and matriculants in either year at any aid level. This seems to indicate that aided state residents find the net price of attendance to be acceptable at whatever aid level they are in, while non-state residents find higher aid awards an attractive reason to matriculate at this institution.

Another way to visualize these conclusions with the same data is to examine the *ratio* of total aid between admits and matrics (Figure 3.5).

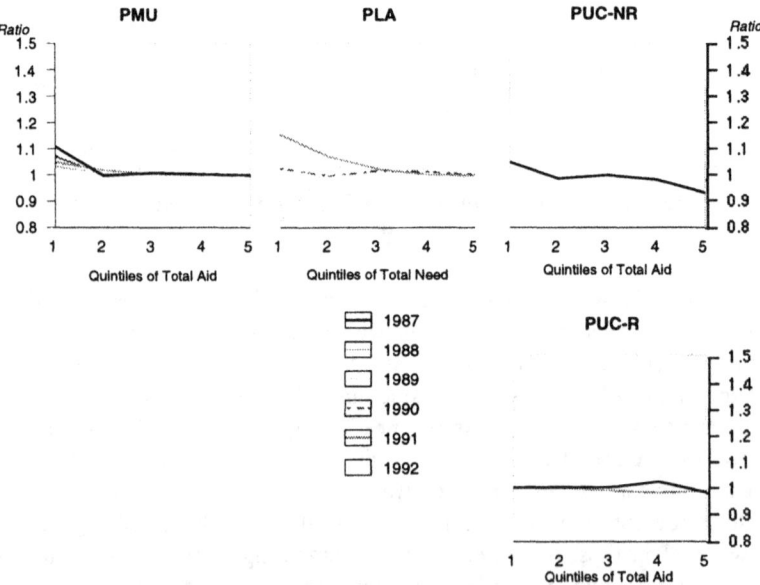

Figure 3.5 - Ratio of Total Aid, Admits to Matrics

A ratio of 1 indicates no difference. Ratios above 1 favor matriculating students; ratios below 1 favor admitted students. The conclusions here concur with the discussion above. The graph of PMU shows some difference in the first quintile of total aid, most pronounced in 1992, and little difference in any other quintile and in any other year. The graph of PLA shows some erratic differences also in the first quintile, and little difference in any other. The graph of non-state residents at PUC clearly shows the trend of favoring matrics slightly in the first quintile of aid, then favoring admits in the fourth and fifth quintiles. The graph of state residents at PUC once again exhibits little difference at all.

3. Aid Packaging

As a way to understand why there may be more price sensitivity in the lower aid levels, the quality of the financial aid packages received by admits and matrics can be examined. The following data detail the percentage of total aid award received by admits and matrics that was "self help" (loans and work). The larger the self help (and therefore the lower the pure grant) component, the worse the aid package is considered to be.

Tables 3.5a through 3.5c show the average amount of self help for admitted students by quintile of the aided population (that is, the first quintile represents the first 20% of aided students, those receiving the least aid). Also shown is the average difference between the amount of self help of the admits and the subset of each quintile that actually matriculated. Data for PLA were not available. Positive numbers in the bottom half of each table indicate that, for those cells, matriculating students on average received better aid awards than admitted students, that is *less* self help. The more positive the numbers the greater the effect of price on the decision to matriculate; if price was not a factor, then the level of self help for matriculating students would be no different on average than the level for admitted students within each aid range (quintile).

		1987	1988	1989	1990	1991	1992
Admits	1	$2,562	$2,781	$3,127	$3,520	$3,726	$3,884
	2	$3,708	$4,194	$4,313	$4,619	$5,052	$5,094
	3	$3,669	$4,189	$4,229	$4,395	$4,917	$4,997
	4	$3,617	$4,097	$4,229	$4,374	$5,047	$4,933
	5	$3,348	$3,827	$3,986	$3,959	$4,554	$4,728
Difference Between Admits and Matrics (Admits - Matrics)	1	($127)	$158	$85	$143	$120	$26
	2	($56)	$96	($22)	$24	$72	$345
	3	($35)	($56)	$112	$107	$251	$296
	4	($3)	($28)	($60)	$37	$103	$228
	5	($49)	($156)	($208)	($60)	($47)	$230

Table 3.5a - Average Amount of Self Help for PMU, by Quintile

		1987	1988	1989	1990	1991	1992
Admits	1					$1,500	$1,613
	2					$3,211	$2,780
	3					$4,639	$3,968
	4					$5,294	$4,047
	5					$4,335	$3,939
Difference Between Admits and Matrics (Admits - Matrics)	1					$89	$114
	2					$257	($43)
	3					$449	$162
	4					$385	$161
	5					$773	$975

Table 3.5b - Average Amount of Self Help for PUC Non-state Residents, by Quintile

		1987	1988	1989	1990	1991	1992
Admits	1					$420	$507
	2					$912	$692
	3					$687	$1,239
	4					$1,161	$2,029
	5					$1,290	$903
Difference Between Admits and Matrics (Admits - Matrics)	1					($49)	$89
	2					($144)	$133
	3					$65	$86
	4					$62	$358
	5					$337	$305

Table 3.5c - Average Amount of Self Help for PUC State Residents, by Quintile

This difference is displayed graphically in Figure 3.6. For PMU, the trend has been for matrics to increasingly have a smaller amount of self help than admits, and therefore a relatively better overall financial aid package. Over the six years for which there are data, not only did matrics receive a lower amount of self help year after year, but the difference increased year after year. Additionally, the difference began to tip in favor of the matrics first in the lower quintiles of aid; then it began to work its way to every quintile of aid. Finally by 1992 matrics in every quintile, on average, had a lower amount of self help in their award packages.

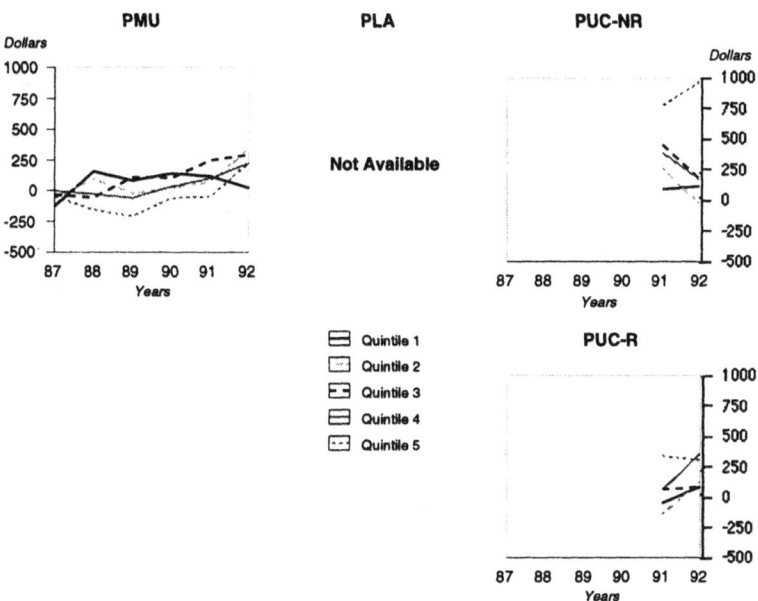

Figure 3.6 - Difference in Amount of Self Help Between Admits and Matrics

For PUC non-state residents, matrics had a lower amount of self help almost exclusively for both years for which there were data. The difference narrowed for most quintiles from 1991 to 1992 except for the last quintile, or those students with the most aid, where the difference was double the fourth quintile and the gap continued to grow. For PUC state residents, the results were much the same, though the differences were much less severe, and the quintiles were more closely clustered together. In 1991 admits were actually favored in the lower quintiles of aid. By 1992, both the fourth and fifth quintiles of aid showed a similar noticeable difference.

Once again, another way to visualize these conclusions with the same data is to examine the *ratio* of self help between admits and matrics (Figure 3.7).

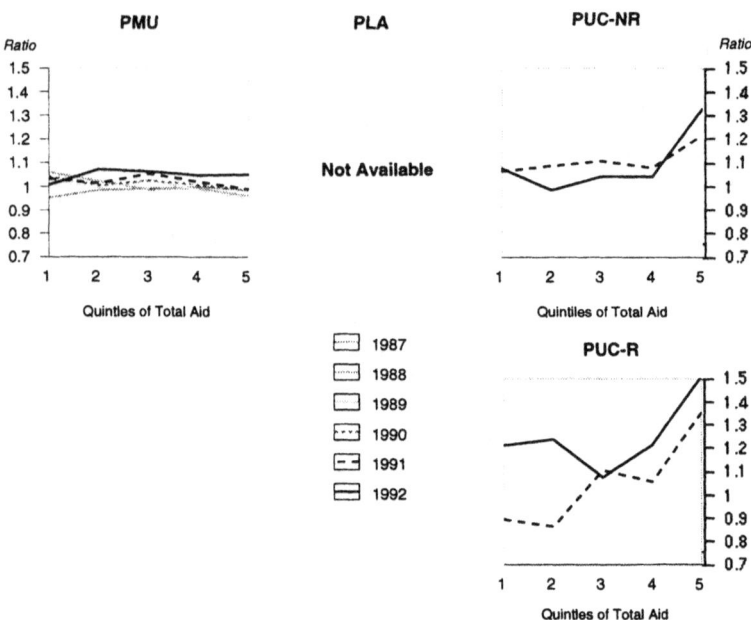

Figure 3.7 - Ratio of Amount of Self Help, Admits to Matrics

A ratio of 1 indicates no difference. Ratios above 1 favor matriculating students; ratios below 1 favor admitted students. The conclusions here concur with the discussion above. The graph of PMU shows generally even spread between admits and matrics among the different quintiles of aid, with admits being favored in 1987 and 1988, while matrics were favored in the later years. The graph of non-state residents at PUC shows the overall trend favoring the matrics, more so in 1991 than 1992, except for the fifth quintile of aid where matrics are even more favored. The graph of state residents at PUC shows the difference between 1991 and 1992 in the lower quintiles, and the consistent increase in difference favoring the matrics in the higher deciles of aid.

Finally, there may be differences in the proportion of total aid award that comes from the self help component. Tables 3.6a through 3.6c show the average proportion of the total aid award that was self

Student Price Sensitivity: Results from Three Schools 69

help for admitted students by quintile of the aided population (that is, the first quintile represents the first 20% of aided students, those receiving the least aid). Also shown is the average difference between the proportion of self help of the admits and the subset of each quintile that actually matriculated. Data for PLA were again not available.

		1987	1988	1989	1990	1991	1992
Admits	1	78.20%	81.94%	78.98%	75.16%	81.82%	80.90%
	2	46.71%	51.64%	47.64%	45.70%	49.04%	46.65%
	3	33.07%	36.49%	33.71%	32.01%	33.99%	32.34%
	4	26.59%	28.71%	27.37%	25.88%	28.45%	26.04%
	5	20.51%	22.09%	21.42%	19.74%	21.40%	20.99%
Difference Between Admits and Matrics (Admits - Matrics)	1	1.57%	7.16%	5.51%	5.83%	6.37%	8.36%
	2	-0.77%	1.63%	0.52%	0.66%	1.51%	2.96%
	3	-0.09%	-0.28%	0.95%	0.75%	1.82%	2.14%
	4	0.06%	-0.12%	-0.37%	0.31%	0.57%	1.24%
	5	-0.24%	-0.85%	-1.16%	-0.25%	-0.17%	0.98%

Table 3.6a - Average Proportion of Total Aid Award that is Self Help for PMU, by Quintile

		1987	1988	1989	1990	1991	1992
Admits	1					85.70%	85.52%
	2					93.31%	94.13%
	3					92.12%	93.90%
	4					89.57%	72.97%
	5					48.02%	43.10%
Difference Between Admits and Matrics (Admits - Matrics)	1					3.23%	2.13%
	2					4.73%	-0.20%
	3					7.51%	3.82%
	4					9.50%	4.09%
	5					10.81%	12.85%

Table 3.6b - Average Proportion of Total Aid Award that is Self Help for PUC Non-state Residents, by Quintile

		1987	1988	1989	1990	1991	1992
Admits	1					39.76%	31.72%
	2					38.82%	23.74%
	3					18.99%	29.01%
	4					22.80%	36.28%
	5					16.59%	11.61%
Difference Between Admits and Matrics (Admits - Matrics)	1					-4.58%	5.62%
	2					-6.08%	4.65%
	3					1.64%	2.08%
	4					0.83%	7.11%
	5					4.20%	3.79%

Table 3.6c - Average Proportion of Total Aid Award that is Self Help for PUC State Residents, by Quintile

Positive numbers in the bottom half of each table indicate that for those cells matriculating students on average received better aid awards than admitted students, that is a *lower* proportion of self help in the overall award. The more positive the numbers the greater the effect of price on the decision to matriculate; if price was not a factor, then the proportion of self help in the awards of matriculating students would be no different on average than the proportion in the awards for admitted students within each aid range (quintile).

This difference is displayed graphically in Figure 3.8.

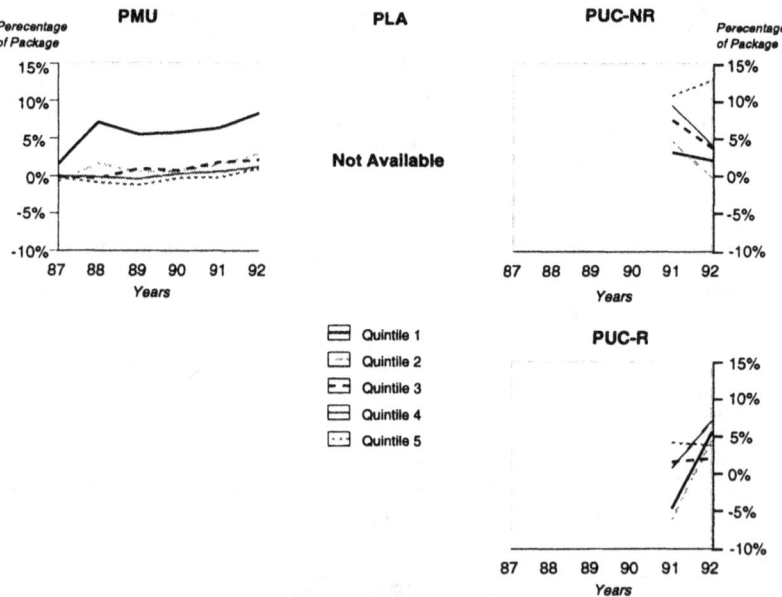

Figure 3.8 - Difference Between Admits and Matrics in the Proportion of Total Aid Award that is Self Help

The graph of PMU shows virtually no difference in the proportion of the total aid award that is self help in anything but the first quintile of aid, where the difference is significant (over 8% by 1992). The graph of non-state residents at PUC shows for 1991 a stratification of packaging, with the difference in the proportion of self help consistently rising as the level of total aid increased. This trend was less severe in 1992 except for the highest aid quintile where the difference in proportion of total aid awards that was self help favoring matrics even more significantly. The graph of state residents at PUC shows, for 1991, admits being favored in the lower aid quintiles, while matrics were favored in the higher aid quintiles. By 1992, matrics were favored in every aid decile, with little difference apparent by aid level.

4. Implications for an Institution In Aggregate

Differences in aid between matrics and admits can have a profound impact on the institution in aggregate. When matrics have a higher level of aid than admits, the estimates of overall aid requirements that an institution prepares can be in error, since these estimates often assume that aided students will matriculate with aid packages at or near the average of the aid packages for their admitted population.

Table 3.7 shows the aggregate difference in total aid between matrics and admits in the sample institutions (missing data are indicated by shaded cells).

	1987	1988	1989	1990	1991	1992	Total
PMU	$76,552	$57,015	$53,505	$67,601	$82,654	$79,125	$416,454
PLA			($1,088)	$25,507	$25,750		$50,170
PUC-NR					$65,999	$77,055	$143,055
PUC-R					($8,777)	$1,080	($7,696)

Table 3.7 - Aggregate Difference in Total Aid Between Admits and Matrics

Positive numbers indicate an additional expense for the institution as the matriculating students were better aided on average than the admitted students. Negative numbers indicate a savings for the institution as the matriculating students had less overall aid on average than admitted students.

Over the six years for which there are data, PMU will expend more than $416,000 than might have otherwise been predicted for aid for its incoming freshman class. This will, of course, ripple through the aid estimates for upper class students as well. PLA will expend just over $50,000 for the three years for which data have been provided.

PUC will expend over $140,000 for the two years for which data are provided for its non-state residents, while saving almost $7,700 on its state residents.

But the story does not end here. It has already been shown that the packaging of this aid also differs from admits to matrics, as Table 3.8 bears out.

	1987	1988	1989	1990	1991	1992	Total
PMU	$53,542	$9,508	$23,393	($44,510)	($91,972)	($222,646)	($272,685)
PLA							
PUC-NR					($237,869)	($150,479)	($388,348)
PUC-R					($12,250)	($45,660)	($57,909)

Table 3.8 - Aggregate Difference in Self Help Between Admits and Matrics

When it comes to self help, matrics at PMU received over $272,000 less self help than might have been predicted from the pool of admits. Non-state resident matrics at PUC received almost $390,000 less in self-help, while state resident matrics at PUC received almost $58,000 less in self-help. Data are not available for PLA.

Table 3.9 displays the cumulative effect of the increase in total aid from Table 3.7 and the decrease in self help from Table 3.8.

	1987	1988	1989	1990	1991	1992	Total
PMU	$23,010	$47,507	$30,112	$112,111	$174,626	$301,771	$689,138
PLA							
PUC-NR					$303,868	$227,534	$531,402
PUC-R					$3,473	$46,740	$50,213

Table 3.9 - Aggregate Difference in Grant Between Admits and Matrics

Over six years, PMU is required to come up with almost $690,000 in grant funds to make up the difference in total aid combined with the difference in self help between admits and matrics! PUC is forced to come up with over $531,000 for its non-state residents, and just over $50,000 for its state residents. Given the limited availability of federal and state financial aid funds, these amounts will likely need to come from precious institutional grant sources.

Implications of the Model

Table 3.10 summarizes the conclusions that can be reached based on the hypotheses developed, and the actual data analyzed through comparing the patterns that exist between the yield levels, aid levels, and aid packaging:

		PMU	PLA	PUC-NR	PUC-R
Yield	Differences in Yield Percentages	M	L	M	M
	Proportion of Population by Student Category	L	L	M	M
	Yield by Quintile of Aid	M	M	L	L
Total Aid	Difference in Average Total Aid Between Admits and Matrics	L	M	L-M	L
	Ratio of Total Aid, Admits to Matrics	L	L-M	L	L
Self Help	Difference in Amount of Self Help Between Admits and Matrics	L-M		M-E	M
	Ratio of Amount of Self Help, Admits to Matrics	L		M-E	E
	Difference in Proportion of Total Aid that is Self Help	L-M		M-E	L-M

Italics indicate change or volitility over time.

Table 3.10 - Summary of Results from Actual Data

The measures in this table indicate the following:

- The private multiversity (PMU) exhibited little price sensitivity overall, though some price sensitivity was found among the least aided students. Little difference appeared over the six years studied, though some effects worsened in the final year (1992).
- The private liberal arts college (PLA) exhibited somewhat stronger price sensitivity than the private multiversity (PMU) both over time and across levels of need, with some apparent intervention on behalf of the institution during the years being studied that was effective in attracting aided students to matriculate.
- The public comprehensive university (PUC) exhibited the most price sensitivity, especially among the non-state residents. Some of the effects seemed to be less evident over time.

Perceptions of the Institutions

How does this evidence compare to the way these institutions perceive their own situation to be vis-a-vis price sensitivity? The appropriate directors of financial aid or admissions at each of the institutions were asked about their perceptions of their own institution, without revealing the hypotheses suggested by the model.

The financial aid director at PMU offered the following insights. Within quintiles of aid, PMU expects differences between admits and matrics to be minimal. Students in the lower quintiles of need should be more sensitive to price than those in the upper quintiles. The yield of lower quintiles of aid will probably be approximately 60% of what might be expected without price sensitivity; the yield of upper quintiles of need will probably be approximately 95% of what might be expected.

PMU believes that yield differences are more a factor of whether students with certain aid profiles have more competing opportunities for admission. Officials there expect to see students with the highest self help have a *higher* yield since they tend to have fewer better choices for admission than at PMU.

When Overlap was in effect, all differences between packages were eliminated. Students who did not apply to other Overlap schools typically had their yield vary with their level of overall aid. Differences in self-help were not terribly significant. Surprisingly, when Overlap was in effect, about 25% of the top students who qualified for need-based aid did not apply to any other Overlap school.

Finally, it would be useful to study student choice of the non-matriculants to see what competing aid awards were, and to see if students will admit if they did not matriculate at PMU due to differences in net price of admission. PMU assumes that any applicant with strong credentials who applies to a lower tier school could likely get merit-based aid.

The vice president of budget and planning at PLA believes that the higher the level of need the more likely a student is to matriculate. Students with little need are unlikely to matriculate. PLA has observed a slight increase over time in non-needy matriculants, though it believes the proportion of these students in the applicant pool has declined. Officials at PLA have observed an increase in the proportion of admitted students eligible for aid, and the level of their eligibility has

Student Price Sensitivity: Results from Three Schools 75

been increasing.

Until the fall 1992 class, aid was awarded based on a need-blind policy, then distributed to all qualifying matriculants regardless of the overall level of the financial aid budget. Over time, PLA believes that middle income students seem be matriculating at a lower rate than they once had.

The dean of admissions at PUC expects to see more price sensitivity among the neediest students, particularly among non-state residents. In addition, he expects the more attractive students to be more sensitive to price than the less attractive students. Finally, since PUC is not able to meet the level of need of all of its students, it expects that the yield for students whose need is not fully met would drop as the gap between aid and need increases.

Assessment of the Model

Which of these measures seem to be good indicators of price sensitivity? Table 3.11 matches the results from the data (summarized in Table 3.10) to the perceptions of the officials from the three institutions.

		Consistent with Institutional perspective of Price Sensitivity?
Yield	Differences in Yield Percentages	√
	Proportion of Population by Student Category	√
	Yield by Quintile of Aid	Not for PUC
Total Aid	Difference in Average Total Aid Between Admits and Matrics	√
	Ratio of Total Aid, Admits to Matrics	√
Self Help	Difference in Amount of Self Help Between Admits and Matrics	√
	Ratio of Amount of Self Help, Admits to Matrics	Not for PUC-R
	Difference in Proportion of Total Aid that is Self Help	√

Table 3.11 - Summary of Data as Compared to Institutional Perception

Most of the measures used provide a view of price sensitivity consistent with the perceptions of the institutions. Some results for PUC are not consistent, in one case understating (yield by quintile of aid) and in another case overstating (ratio of self help) the level of price sensitivity that is exhibited in the university. Given that the perceptions of the officials are otherwise consistent with the data (to the degree that comments were offered), these two inconsistencies are anomalies in the data.

Conclusions

Any college or university should be able to articulate its perceptions about price sensitivity, then look at its own data and perform an analysis similar to the one conducted in this chapter to verify or disprove the degree to which price is a factor in the decisions of their students to matriculate. The next chapter will begin to frame a possible solution to managing this price sensitivity in the institution.

Notes

1. Carnegie Commission on Higher Education, *A Classification of Institutions of Higher Education* (New York: McGraw-Hill, 1973).
2. J. Victor Baldridge et al., *Policy Making and Effective Leadership* (San Francisco: Jossey-Bass, 1983), pp. 58-61.
3. As Table 3.1 shows, there were too few students who were needy and unaided to include this data in the analysis for PMU. Given that this institution practiced "need blind admissions" for all of the years included, these few cases of needy and unaided students are likely to be anomalies in the data.
4. In this figure and all that follow, PUC-NR indicates the non-state resident students of this university; PUC-R indicates the state residents.
5. PUC is a state institution that does not practice need-blind admissions. In addition, unsubsidized student or parent loan programs, like SLS and Plus Loans, may have been included in the calculated aid award by the institution but were excluded for the purpose of this analysis.
6. In the case of PLA, once again, total need is being used as a surrogate for total aid.

IV
Banking Functions

Introduction

Once a college or university identifies and understands price sensitivity among its students, as the model in Chapter 2 and sample institutional analyses in Chapter 3 display, it needs to find strategies to reduce the net price of attendance for those price sensitive students it wishes to attract. More than likely, institutions will need to find ways to increase the funds available for price discounting (financial aid), or find new ways to help students and their families better afford the price of attendance.

This chapter will begin to define and discuss the Academic Bank whose goal is to provide some structure and stability to support innovative approaches to student financing for colleges and universities with price sensitive students. In this chapter, the set of broad functions performed by banks will first be discussed. Next, a framework for classifying financial services institutions will be developed, and different types of banks will be defined. Lastly, questions and issues regarding the unique qualities of the Academic Bank will be raised.

Modern Banking Functions[1]

Banks perform two major functions: transaction services and financial intermediation. Transaction services enable or facilitate cash transactions. Banks convert assets held in deposits to cash, and perform inter-account and inter-bank transfers to settle debts (payment services). Well over three quarters of all financial transactions (by volume, not value) in the United States are still by exchange of cash, with checks and account transfers following. Banks are active in all three of these types of transactions either directly with checks and transfers or indirectly as depository institutions whose deposits are available on demand and frequently called upon in cash transactions. Other transaction services include the convenient exchange of one currency type for another, the provision of automated clearing houses for checks, electronic fund transfers, wire transfers, and credit card services.

Banks historically did not charge for transaction services on a transaction by transaction basis, though recently this has begun to change. Transaction, and particularly payment, services are usually accomplished with funds held in deposit accounts which by law cannot have interest paid on their holdings. Banks, however, are not required to retain all of the funds deposited in demand accounts at all times (referred to as fractional reserve banking in the United States). They can invest, or loan, these funds and receive earnings to compensate them for providing transaction services. The cost of providing these services is the same for each transaction regardless of the size of the transaction. Some banks today have begun charging fees for transactions, often for the number of transactions processed within a specific time period beyond a certain minimum number. Any transaction, of course, takes place between two parties, often in different banks. Part of the resistance of banks to charging transaction fees is their inability to determine and collect the portion of the true transaction cost that should be paid by the other party.

Financial intermediation, the second of the two major functions of banks, refers to the positioning of the banking institution between lenders and borrowers of capital, and the performance of a variety of services for a fee. One service performed by banks is a brokerage function. Banks bring parties together by providing better information and convenience in accomplishing a transaction that the parties could not have achieved as easily alone. This service does not involve the creation of any new assets, but merely "matchmaking" between potential borrowers and lenders.

A second service is portfolio transformation, which is the creation of new types of assets offered to borrowers that are substantially altered versions of the original assets acquired by the bank. Often this is accomplished by pooling the assets of various types of investments and offering portions to other investors. Mutual funds are probably the best example of this type of intermediation service, where a wide variety of assets are acquired with various maturity dates and at various rates of interest with the funds of many small investors who buy "shares" in the group of assets. Most likely, the small- to medium-size investor would not be able to acquire similar assets without the help of an intermediary due to the high minimum purchase amount.

A third intermediation service is the provision of guarantees to facilitate financing between parties. These guarantees use the reputation of the intermediary to help one or both parties accomplish a transaction.

Usually, this service involves the use of off-balance sheet, contingent liabilities that may never be called upon, but which provide some type of insurance for one or both parties.

Implicit in all of these intermediation services is the sharing of risk by the bank with other parties. The bank, of course, charges a fee for assuming part of the risk. Normally, this fee is represented by the difference between the interest charged to the borrowers and the interest paid to the providers of capital. The provision of transaction services also involves risk to the bank. Particularly with respect to check processing, and to a lesser degree with electronic fund transfers, there is always the risk that funds that need to flow into the bank will not be available when demanded. Different banks develop different policies and procedures to minimize this risk, usually by restricting to the customer the availability of funds to be collected from other banks until the funds are actually retrieved. Recent regulation has begun to limit the amount of time banks may withhold a depositor's access to newly-deposited funds.

Financial Services Institutions

Creating an exact definition of a bank is difficult. The Bank Holding Company Act defines and uses "bank" to mean "commercial bank."[2] Anything else is a "non-bank bank". A more functional definition is preferred, which looks at the services performed and the customers served in the context of the functions described above. Figure 4.1 displays the types of financial services institutions in the United States. The left side of the figure deals with banking institutions; the right side deals with non-bank banks. In this framework, institution types that clearly provide both transaction and intermediation services together to some broad constituency are defined as banks. The transaction services must include a demand deposit account, or a close functional equivalent (*e.g.* NOW accounts). Any institution types that offer either transaction or intermediation services, but not both (typically the latter), are classified as non-bank banks. The status of the Academic Bank has yet to be determined.

While non-bank banks perform financial services functions they are outside of the regulatory constraints of the banking industry. They are also more focused in the services they perform. Before the Academic Bank can be fully understood, the similarities and differences between these different kinds of banks and non-bank banks must be explained.

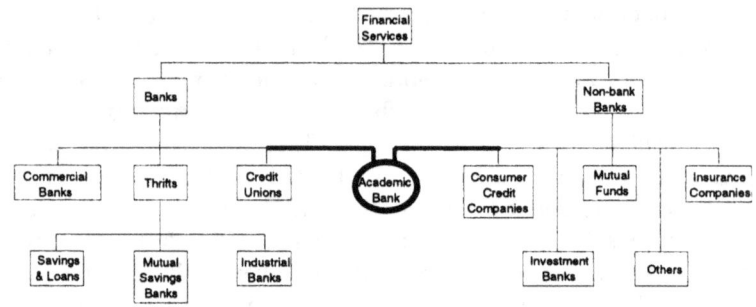

Figure 4.1 - Types of Financial Services Institutions

Over the past twenty years particularly, the differences between all of these types of institutions have been reduced dramatically. In most cases it is due to the continued deregulation of the banking industry. Through a variety of legislative efforts whose momentum is only slowing now, the restrictions placed upon the services offered by non-commercial banks have all but disappeared. Non-bank banks have been allowed to diversify their services into areas historically reserved to banking institutions, or to each other. While this diversification has brought many of these industries away from their original, primary lines of business, it has not always been by choice. In part, these ancillary services were developed for the customer's convenience to minimize either the time or cost to the customer of searching and information gathering in accomplishing financial objectives. In some cases, diversification was purely a defensive move by an industry or firm in response to another industry moving into its primary service.

In many ways, a bank's primary asset is its relationship to its customers, and the information that is accumulated during the course of a customer's relationship with the bank. Financial services firms, including banks, have at times preferred to provide either transaction or intermediation services to their customers, but not both. It has typically been customers who have demanded that intermediaries provide payment services for their convenience. In the case of non-bank banks, it has been the need to invest or loan funds held on deposit to cover transaction costs that has required them to perform intermediation as well. In addition to these customer-inspired pressures to diversify, transaction services companies have also realized that the provision of transaction services allows the accumulation of sufficient information to develop customer profiles which prove invaluable in providing credit in the form of loans.

Types of Banks

As Figure 4.1 details, there are three basic types of banks in the United States: commercial banks, thrifts, and credit unions. Commercial banks and thrifts represent the two most dominant and most important types of banks existing in the United States today. Each represents a segment of the industry whose lines of separation have become obscured. Commercial banks are best known for performing wholesale banking, and thrifts are best known for retail banking. Both involve the combination of transaction and intermediation services in one institution. But, while retail banking primarily exists to service many small individual and business customers with a large volume of low-value transactions, wholesale banks exist to service a small number of very large commercial customers and government authorities. Their basic functions are the same, though they accomplish them with slightly different means.[3]

Customers of retail banks demand liquidity, that is the ability to change the money they have on deposit in the bank to currency on demand. Much of what banks do in the form of transaction services is to establish and reinforce the confidence of its customers in the ultimate liquidity of the bank. Of course, banks are not 100% liquid. The system of fractional reserve banking in the United States allows banks to only hold a portion of their demand deposits liquid, and use the rest for interest-generating activities.

Typically, retail banks have many deposit accounts of varying types, none of which are particularly large in comparison to total deposits. The retail bank usually holds reserves in excess of the amount required by law. The bank's true business is, of course, making loans.[4] The interest collected on loans is almost always greater than the transaction fees and charges collected. The fees and charges usually do not even cover the expenses that the transactions themselves generate. Usually, many customers of a retail bank have loans of varying types, again none of which is terribly large in relation to the total of all loans. These loans have varying maturities and interest rates. The information compiled about a customer concerning his/her transactions processed by the bank usually identifies customers who represent good credit risks to the bank.

Besides using money from deposits to generate loans, banks also create additional liabilities by borrowing, usually at short-term interest rates, and then lending the same money at long-term rates. This process, referred to as "positive maturity transformation," creates a profit potential for the bank as long as the short-term interest rates at which the funds are borrowed are lower than the long-term rates at which the same funds are loaned to the customers. More recent developments that assist banks in making these situations profitable are the rise of variable-rate loans, and the development of secondary markets for loans, that both add additional protection to the bank and lower interest rate risk. Variable rate loans pass more interest rate risk directly to the customer, while secondary markets allow other avenues for the bank to use in getting rid of unfavorable assets.

Retail banks also face another kind of risk in addition to interest rate risk—asset risk. This is the risk posed by bad borrowers who either prove to be unwilling or unable to repay their loans. Banks try to control this risk as much as possible through careful credit checks and scrutiny. Depending on the overall economy, credit can be either very tight or very loose, exposing the bank to greater potential asset risk when credit is in the latter situation.

Yet another kind of risk is withdrawal risk, which is the possibility at any time of any customer demanding that funds be withdrawn from a demand account. The risk is real only to the degree that the bank has insufficient cash reserves to satisfy the request for funds. Continued development of electronic funds transfers, and regional, national and international clearinghouses for financial transactions, will increase the likelihood that the demand for funds by one customer will be matched almost instantaneously by the inflow of funds for another.

Wholesale banks follow the same basic principles as retail banks, only they tend to have very few customers since the customers represent very large accounts. Because of the size of the customers, transactions tend to be very large as well, as does intermediation.

Banking Functions

Typically, the interest rate margins are not as wide as in retail banking, but the size of the transactions usually makes up for this deficiency. Unlike retail banks, wholesale banks usually have loans in excess of their deposits. This is accomplished through "pooling" with other wholesale banks and performing loan syndication, where the collective strength of several banks is used to support the creation of a new loan asset for all of them. This notion is similar to co-insurance and reinsurance in the insurance industry, where firms collectively issue a large policy, or reinsure a risky policy with another insurance company.

Wholesale banks strive for a balance in their maturity structure, that is they strive to achieve the perfect situation of having loans of a particular maturity financed by deposits of the same maturity. Because of the relatively small number of customers, wholesale banks use each other to create this balance by "borrowing" the necessary deposits to support the loans they want to make. They also make much greater use of secondary markets to manage their asset portfolios by selling loans that they feel no longer have deposits of similar maturity with which to balance. On the liability side, wholesale banks hold certificates of deposit, and/or reserve funds purchased from the Federal Reserve to help balance loans they wish to retain.

Therefore, while retail banks (primarily thrifts) use large numbers of depositors to develop reserves, wholesale banks (primarily commercial banks) use syndication to spread risk. Banking is essentially, after all, an insurance business. Reserves are held in support of full payment of deposit liabilities that should never have to be paid all at one time. Wholesale banks also use off-balance sheet activities to further generate fees for contingent liabilities they gamble will never be called upon.

It should be made clear that commercial banks certainly have always had retail customers, and thrifts have always had commercial customers, even large ones who, ordinarily, one might expect to find at a commercial (*i.e.* wholesale) bank. Typically, however, commercial banks have not pursued retail customer accounts, and have historically chosen to establish few non-commercial loans. Thrifts have generally been founded to appeal to the retail customer and have chosen to focus their energy on that market.

A typical simplified balance sheet and income statement for a wholesale or retail bank looks as follows[5]:

Balance Sheet

Assets	Liabilities
Cash Reserves 　Required 　Excess	Deposits Other borrowing
Marketable securities	Shareholder's equity
Loans to customers	
Physical capital	

Income Statement

Income	Expense
Interest Earnings	Operating Expenses
Fees and charges	Interest paid
	Profit (transferred to shareholders)

Commercial banks are clearly the most powerful banks in the United States, economically in terms of the assets they control, and politically. They can be chartered at either the national or state level. Nationally-chartered commercial banks have agreed to accept the regulatory authority of the Federal government, while state-chartered banks have opted to accept state regulation only. State-chartered banks may additionally accept elements of Federal regulation that go along with specific benefits, such as Federal deposit insurance. The definition of a commercial bank is an institution which, in the words of the Bank Holding Company Act, " . . . (1) accepts demand deposits or deposits that the depositor may withdraw by check or similar means for payment to third parties or others; and (2) engages in the business of making commercial loans."[6]

There are several types of thrift institutions, the most popular one being the savings and loan, also chartered either at the national or state level. These institutions are primarily founded to finance primary home mortgages. Because regulation of these institutions is nonspecific in many jurisdictions, savings and loan institutions have also engaged in a variety of other activities.[7] A recent trend of deregulation has left savings and loans, as well as other thrifts, extremely competitive with commercial banks and money market funds (see below). The Depository Institutions Deregulation and Monetary Control Act of 1980 was the most significant, making the rules that apply to all depository institutions fairly uniform. This included universal access to Federal Reserve System services, the ability to offer checking accounts, and the ability for savings and loans to offer credit cards and a greater variety of consumer loans.[8] The Garn-St Germain Act of 1982 followed shortly. On the liability side of the balance sheet, not only did it allow thrift institutions to offer to their customers unlimited checking accounts, it allowed them to pay an unregulated amount of interest on these accounts with balances of as little as $2,500. This act also allowed thrifts to create money market accounts with balances as low as $2,500 as well (the minimum was subsequently eliminated). On the asset side of the balance sheet, thrifts were granted much more freedom to invest in government securities and a greater variety of loans.[9]

A variety of state-only-chartered thrifts exist as well. Mutual savings banks are most popular in the Northeast, and are primarily savings institutions providing productive, long-term investments for their depositors. Deposits are usually in the form of regular savings accounts, and the banks are considered debtors to their depositors. Savings banks can also extend a variety of credit services, depending on the jurisdiction, though they usually concentrate on primary home mortgages.[10] The Depository Institutions Deregulation and Monetary Control Act benefited mutual savings banks particularly, allowing them to make business loans and create checking accounts for business customers.[11] Some states allow the chartering of industrial banks, or thrifts and loans, whose origin was providing savings and credit services to industrial workers (thus their name). Unlike savings and loans, a greater variety of credit services are normally available from industrial banks.[12]

Credit unions have developed as associations of individuals whose primary purpose is to save and provide credit for their members. Credit unions are chartered at either the national or state level.[13] Regulatory changes initiated in 1978 have enabled credit unions to issue primary home mortgages of any size for any maturity, offering some real competition to savings and loans. Credit unions have offered competition to commercial banks as well, particularly by being in the forefront of innovation with services like payroll deduction plans, debit and credit cards, and loan insurance.[14]

Types of Non-bank Banks

The other group of financial services institutions that exist in the United States are referred to as non-bank banks. They are banks in that they perform many of the functions discussed above, though usually either transaction services or intermediation. They are not technically banks, however, because they are not depository institutions, and because they do not fall under the banking regulations of either the Federal or state governments. They are subject to other regulation of various kinds, from consumer credit protection to regulation by the Securities and Exchange Commission. These non-bank banks have been increasingly moving in practice towards banking.

Consumer finance companies developed in the early twentieth century as non-depository institutions offering consumer credit under state regulation.[15] Often these companies were outgrowths of manufacturing or sales organizations that found that by disintermediating banks from the financing of their sales by their customers they could add to their overall profits, and offer superior convenience to their customers by providing "one-stop shopping" for both their products and the funds to finance purchases. General Motors, Sears, and Ford Motor Company have been among the largest retail lenders in the country for some time.[16]

Consumer credit companies exploited an opportunity left untapped by commercial banks—the consumer credit market. It was not until after World War II that commercial banks took a real interest in consumer credit. By now, consumer credit companies have such a hold on this market that they pose a serious threat to the commercial lending market as well. Still other consumer credit companies have grown out of related capital-generating businesses like insurance and real estate, and coupled themselves with them.[17]

Why was expansion into banking functions so attractive? In part, the answer lies in the impressive profits that banks have historically earned, as well as banks' good showing in developing healthy asset increases year in and year out even in times of recession. For some companies, weakness in their primary products or services forced them into diversification.[18]

The 1970's brought one great contribution to the financial services market—money market mutual funds, the second type of non-bank banks. These non-bank banks thrived during a time of very high interest rates coupled with federal rules in the form of the Federal Reserve's Regulation Q that placed ceilings on the interest rates that banking institutions could pay to their customers. Mutual funds are technically not depository in nature. Rather, customers purchase shares in the fund which have a set value. The return on the investment is made either through the purchase of new shares or through the periodic disbursement of funds directly to the customer. In this way, mutual funds have stayed outside of the regulatory jurisdiction of the banking industry.[19]

Because the funds tended to be "no-load" funds (*i.e.* they had no explicit transaction charges or commissions), they became very attractive to customers. Purchases were easy, even done through electronic funds transfer. In time, money market funds began offering limited transaction services, including check writing against the balance in the fund. Recently, mutual funds have proliferated, developing to a point where specialized funds now exist which cater to an investor's particular public policy goals or social values. Of course, the Depository Institutions Deregulation and Monetary Control Act of 1980, and the Garn-St Germain Depository Institutions Act of 1982 have both made banks more competitive in the money market mutual fund market.

The third type of non-bank banks are insurance companies. Besides offering term life insurance policies, they offer whole life and universal life policies that accumulate value as time goes on that exceeds the face value of the policy. These funds, which usually accumulate tax-free, can be used to secure a loan, or are payable after the term of the policy. Besides making insurance-related investments, insurance companies have diversified into a whole host of financial services. They have also begun to invest in loans in secondary markets (and in savings and loan institutions for that matter) with the plentiful cash that their primary businesses generate.

The fourth kind of non-bank banks are investment banks. The

Glass-Steagall/Banking Act of 1933 created a fairly unique situation in the United States as compared to most industrialized nations: the separation of commercial and investment banking. While commercial banks perform most of the payment and intermediation services discussed above, they are restricted from investment banking activities. That is, they are not allowed to underwrite or broker corporate securities. Similarly, investment banks are restricted from becoming charted as commercial banks. That is, they are not allowed to take deposits or make commercial loans.[20]

Investment banks intermediate the purchase of corporate securities by the public. The process normally has three steps: origination, risk-bearing, and distribution. In the first phase, the investment bank works with the company to determine the appropriate type, quantity, timing, and market for a security. In the risk-bearing phase, the investment bank buys the issue at a fixed price and prepares to sell it to the public. The bank is at risk at this time since the ultimate sale may not materialize. The final phase, distribution, involves the actual sale of the issue to the public.[21]

While there have been no concrete movements by Congress to change the current restrictions imposed by the Glass-Steagall Act, many believe that it is high time for the separation of investment and commercial banking in the United States to end. The traditional belief is that investment banking is inherently riskier than commercial banking, leaving any commercial bank too disposed to insolvency.[22] Critics argue, however, that while underwriting can be risky, steps can be taken to make it no more risky than commercial lending.[23]

A variety of other kinds of companies in non-financial industries have begun to enter the financial services business in significant numbers, and with significant volume. Recently, AT&T has begun to offer a credit card to anyone on the open market, though their own telecommunications customers are being especially targeted. Companies like General Electric and IBM are starting to offer mutual funds of their own. GMAC is now even offering a certificate of deposit that is federally insured. What is interesting about these new endeavors is that the non-financial services firms are usually offering their new services either to their pre-existing retail customer base, or to their sufficiently large employee and retiree populations.[24]

Comparison of Banks and Non-bank Banks

Banks are different from non-bank banks in several important ways. The characteristics of their liabilities tend to be different because of the existence of deposits, especially demand deposits, and the unpredictability of customer requirements for payment services. The characteristics of their assets are also slightly different, in that through the process of making loans they are creating new assets out of old ones. Mutual funds perform the same function of asset creation, but they do not do it through the creation of loans.[25] Insurance companies are like banks in that they take deposits in the form of premiums, invest them, and provide a return through refunds at the end of the contract or death benefits, depending on the type of contract.[26] They do not, however, have demand deposits, and their time deposits are usually of a long duration.

Banks are still by and large more efficient financial institutions than these other types of firms. They gain strength from providing both transaction and intermediation services which customers usually demand for their own convenience. From a systemic point of view, they are better creators of credit because the money created when a loan is made by a bank is likely to always stay within the banking system on deposit in some member institution. When non-bank financial intermediaries create credit, their funds more than likely end up in the banking system deposited in the account of the borrower and out of the intermediaries' hands altogether.[27]

The Academic Bank

Different types of banking institutions develop their customer bases and markets in different ways. Credit unions are by definition groups of individuals with some commonalty or organizational link. Savings banks primarily hold savings accounts and issue home mortgages. Commercial banks attempt to offer comprehensive services, but are really in the market to create credit. Banks try to offer convenience to their customers, and through the somewhat costly processing of transactions, gather information about their customers and their potential needs for the services offered, particularly credit services.

The level of price sensitivity, and among which types of students price sensitivity is being observed, is an important factor in determining a college or university's strategy in creating an Academic Bank. A major component in understanding price sensitivity is understanding the mix of financial aid being awarded to needy students. This mix affects which kinds of banking functions are more appropriate, and therefore what the Academic Bank will look like for a given college or university.

Higher education institutions need to use their own competitive advantage if they are to develop bank-like functions. The challenge is to understand the needs, then to develop the proper sources and mechanisms for deposits, and the proper markets for creating credit. Should the revenue be generated primarily through intermediation services, by identifying unique opportunities for brokering credit arrangements between holders of capital, or through the provision of transaction services? Academic institutions need to identify special customer bases with unique, clearly marketable "mechanisms of convenience." All of this must be done within the bounds of the institution's academic mission.

Should a college or university simply buy a bank? Anderson writes about universities pursuing entrepreneurial activities, even taxable activities, if the overall revenue of the institution increases. Of course, such endeavors should be within an acceptable level of financial, management, and "image" risk.[28] As long as the bank is not a commercial bank (as defined by the Bank Holding Company Act), the University will not be considered a bank holding company and will therefore be outside of the regulatory control of the Federal government.

Regardless of whether a college or university buys, or simply functions as, a bank, the Academic Bank must be able to market itself clearly and favorably. With the increased scrutiny by the public at large of the financial picture of higher education in America, the Academic Bank must be framed in terms that are consistent with the predominant public policy of our times. For this reason, the issue of student aid should be the primary motivator in determining both the proper market for the sources of capital and the proper market for the creation of credit. With the national problems of inadequate college savings and long-term savings, and the real reduction in the availability of federal financial aid in particular, this focus is consistent with institutional and public policy needs.

Banking Functions 93

Summary

Many kinds of institutions, and at an increasing rate non-financial-services firms, are becoming banks and non-bank banks either by providing transaction services, intermediation services, or both. These banking functions are most effectively, though not exclusively, performed by banks. It is hypothesized that academic institutions can use their comparative advantage in certain markets to use banking functions more extensively to assist in solving the worsening student aid problem as part of their fight against student price sensitivity.

Notes

1. For this section I rely largely on Mervyn K. Lewis and Kevin T. Davis, *Domestic and International Banking* (Cambridge, MA: MIT Press, 1987).
2. 12 U.S.C. 1841 (c)(4)(B), and see discussion below.
3. Once again, in the following discussion I rely primarily on Lewis and Davis, and additionally on Kerry Cooper and Donald R. Fraser, *Banking Deregulation and the New Competition in Financial Services* (Cambridge, MA: Ballinger Publishing, 1984), unless otherwise noted.
4. This becomes extremely clear particularly from more practical guides to banking, such as John A. Cook and Robert Wool's *All You Need to Know About Banks* (New York: Bantam, 1983).
5. Adapted from Lewis and Davis, p. 55.
6. 12 U.S.C. 1841 (c)(1)(B).
7. Sheldon Feldman and Kimberly A. Reiley, *A Compilation of Federal and State Laws Regulating Consumer Financial Services* (West Lafayette, IN: Purdue Research Foundation, 1977), p. 675.
8. Cooper and Fraser, p. 116.
9. *Ibid.*, pp. 133-6.
10. Feldman and Reiley, p. 736.
11. Cooper and Fraser, p. 116.
12. Feldman and Reiley, p. 792.
13. *Ibid.*, p. 698.
14. Peter S. Rose, *The Changing Structure of American Banking* (New York: Columbia University Press, 1987), p. 312.
15. Feldman and Reiley, p. 814-5.
16. Cooper and Fraser, p. 199.
17. Rose, pp. 330-2.
18. *Ibid.*, pp. 334-5.
19. *Ibid.*, pp. 312-3.
20. Thomas A. Pugel and Lawrence J. White, "An Analysis of the Competitive Effects of Allowing Commercial Bank Affiliates to Underwrite Corporate Securities" in *Deregulating Wall Street: Commercial Bank Penetration of the Corporate Securities Market*, Ingo Walter, ed. (New York: John Wiley & Sons, 1985), p. 93.
21. *Ibid.*, p. 94.

22. Thomas F. Huertas, Comment on Thomas A. Pugel and Lawrence J. White, "An Analysis of the Competitive Effects of Allowing Commercial Bank Affiliates to Underwrite Corporate Securities" in *Deregulating Wall Street: Commercial Bank Penetration of the Corporate Securities Market*, Ingo Walter, ed. (New York: John Wiley & Sons, 1985), p. 93.

23. Ian H. Giddy, "Is Equity Underwriting Risky for Commercial Bank Affiliates?" in *Deregulating Wall Street: Commercial Bank Penetration of the Corporate Securities Market*, Ingo Walter, ed. (New York: John Wiley & Sons, 1985), pp. 164-5.

24. Glenn Burkins, "Look at Who's in the Financial-Services Business Now," *The Philadelphia Inquirer* (15 July 1990), p. 1-E.

25. Lewis and Davis, pp. 182-3.

26. *Ibid.*, p. 41.

27. *Ibid.*, pp. 187-8.

28. Richard E. Anderson, "Doing Good and Doing Well: A Review of the Entrepreneurial Activities of Colleges and Universities," *Capital Ideas* 5(1 & 2) (New York: National Center for Postsecondary Governance and Finance, June, 1990).

V
The Academic Bank

Introduction

In the previous chapter, the major functions performed by banks and non-bank banks were defined: deposit acceptance, transaction services, and intermediation services. Each bank and non-bank bank performs some or all of these functions, and has certain other specific characteristics, such as the tendency to work with different types of customers, accept certain types of deposits, or make certain types of loans or investments.

But exactly what might the Academic Bank be? It would be a type of banking institution created by a college or university primarily to further institutional goals. The major institutional goal satisfied by the Academic Bank is providing funds for internal investment in student financial aid. In the process, the Academic Bank provides general social benefit by increasing the overall level of savings for college in the community.

The Academic Bank fulfills these goals by performing a series of functions for its constituents. Figure 5.1 summarizes in a matrix the set of Academic Bank functions (vertical axis) and bank and non-bank bank structures from the previous chapter (horizontal axis). Other than providing for college savings, the remaining five functions represent mechanisms for providing a variety of options in student financial aid and student financial services. In reviewing the Academic Bank goals and banking structures it becomes clear that the cells in the matrix are clustered in two areas. This clustering is highlighted by the shading. The first three Academic Bank goals (college savings, providing loans, and funding loans) provide very nice complements to each other when implemented together. College savings provides the necessary capital, while providing and funding loans provides the necessary investments consistent with public policy to make use of college savings dollars until they are required by the depositors. This coupling allows funds accumulating as savings intended for future reductions in family contribution for college by one set of individuals to be used as capital for price discounts of various kinds for current students. As Chapter 4 showed, banking provides the mechanisms to achieve this innovative functionality for higher education.

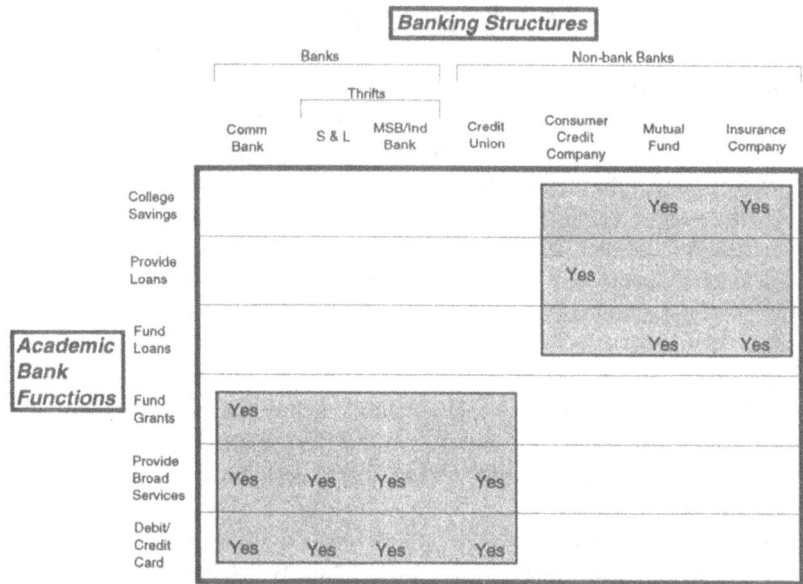

Figure 5.1 - Academic Bank Functions and Banking Structures

For an Academic Bank to fulfill the last three goals (funding grants, providing broad financial services, and providing a debit/credit card) a substantial financial services infrastructure, as well as powerful financial services institutions, are required. Providing a debit/credit card will likely be included by many institutions in their set of broad financial services. Because the capital required to provide the services necessary to satisfy these goals is in most cases substantial, more conventional banking structures are best suited to accomplish them. Higher education may or may not be able to add value to the set of services the commercial banking industry already offers in these areas.

This clustering suggests that there may be two Academic Banks, one focused on using capital accumulated through college savings programs to provide and fund financial aid loans to students, while the other is a full-service institution whose goal it is to provide a broad suite of student financial services. These two Academic Banks could function jointly as one entity if necessary.

But why has the Academic Bank not yet been created? One could argue that it is the very nature of the mix of these functions and services represented in the two shaded areas of Figure 5.1 that has prevented the Academic Bank from being created on college and university campuses so far. Similarly one could argue that higher education financial planners simply did not conceive of such an entity existing on their campuses. Yet another possibility is that the Academic Bank in the past has not been considered appropriate for higher education.

All of these are true. However, these arguments fail to point out the most significant reason: in the past decades colleges and universities have been alarmed by two significant potential restrictions.

The first potential restriction is government regulation. While on the surface the Academic Bank may seem like a reasonable and simple undertaking, it will not be as easy as it appears. Before an implementation can be successful, the many complex legal, regulatory, and social issues need to be solved. These issues are being aggravated by the current feeling of skepticism on the part of many Americans toward both higher education and the financial services industry, banking in particular. The regulatory issues span multiple domains, from securities and exchange to banking, consumer credit to Internal Revenue.

An additional layer of complexity arises from the intertwining of Federal, state and sometimes municipal law that is a part of every business endeavor in the United States. Colleges and universities are no different than any other organization in wanting as little government regulation, and the interference it brings, as possible. Already the benefits of Federal research dollars bring with them increased regulation, scrutiny, and negotiations that are both costly to administer and divert from the primary missions of the institutions.

The second potential restriction is even more feared on the campus: possible jeopardy to the tax exempt status of the college or university itself. The fear of generating what the Internal Revenue Service calls "unrelated business income" from revenue generating activities outside of the tax exempt mission of the organization keeps colleges and universities from being creative financially. However, colleges and universities must be willing to confront the complex regulatory and legal issues that come before them as they consider new financial mechanisms to satisfy institutional goals. Anderson has already written about universities pursuing entrepreneurial activities, even taxable activities, if the overall revenue of the institution increases. Of course, such endeavors should be within an acceptable level of financial, management, and "image" risk.[1]

The balance of this chapter will build on this initial framework and begin to construct the Academic Bank in detail. After describing the series of functions which the Academic Bank might perform, these functions will be examined against the variety of bank and non-bank bank structures identified in the previous chapter.

Academic Bank Functions

The Academic Bank performs one or more of a series of functions for the college or university with which it is affiliated. Figure 5.2 summarizes in a matrix the combinations of banking functions from the previous chapter (vertical axis) that are necessary to accomplish individual Academic Bank functions (horizontal axis).

Banking Functions	**Academic Bank Functions**					
	College Savings	Provide Loans	Fund Loans	Fund Grants	Provide Broad Services	Debit/ Credit Card
Deposit Acceptance	Yes		Yes	Yes	Yes	Yes**
Transaction Services				Yes*	Yes	Yes
Intermediation Services	Portfolio Transformation	Brokerage Services	Portfolio Transformation	Brokerage Services/ Portfolio Transformation	Brokerage Services	Brokerage Services**

* may be required to attract depositors   ** may be required

Figure 5.2 - Banking Functions and Academic Bank Functions

The groupings of these functions, as suggested previously by the shading in Figure 5.1, may indicate that different versions of the Academic Bank may exist to allow a college or university to focus on different institutional goals.

The first function of the Academic Bank is finding ways to further *savings for college*. Remember that this function is necessary primarily to provide capital to finance other functions that further institutional goals. Purdue University's Division of Financial Aid conducted a survey of the parents of current and prospective students. When asked about savings for college, 49% of the parents of current Purdue students, and 52% of the parents of prospective students indicated that they did not save at all for their children's education.[2] Of those parents who did save, barely one half with children currently attending began saving when their children were in junior high school or before, and only 46% of the parents of prospective students began saving when their children were in junior high school or before.[3] Recent studies in Minnesota and Indiana suggest that families believe they have the responsibility to pay for their children's college educations, but that government should provide mechanisms and opportunities to make saving easier.[4]

Americans do not know how to save, and they certainly do not know how to save for college. Families need to find new sources of financing, and need to learn early how to save effectively for college and graduate/professional education with the proper incentives from the government. Since the early 1970's, personal savings in the United States has dropped significantly as a percentage of GNP, and although business savings as a percentage of GNP has shown an upward trend since the end of World War II, it has declined since the mid-1980's.[5] Equally disturbing is the degree to which citizens in some of our competitor nations, Japan especially, are saving at a rate higher than that in the United States.[6]

Savings is a tricky business. Many believe that the tax system provides disincentives for savings while encouraging immediate consumption. While earnings spent on consumable goods or services are taxed only once, at the time they are earned, funds saved or invested are usually taxed again when they generate income. Thus the reward for saving is significantly reduced.[7]

Saving for college is an even trickier business. Should parents accumulate funds in their names or in their child's? Do increased assets decrease the amount of financial aid for which a student will qualify? Predicting either financial aid availability or financial aid policy into the future is hard enough for financial aid specialists, let alone parents.

Other families simply do not know when or how to begin saving, and are more than a little scared about the prospect of affording a $100,000 college education in the year 2000. What is clear, however, is that saving for college makes better financial sense than borrowing to finance college. Since a family earns interest while saving, and pays interest when borrowing, less overall consumption is sacrificed when saving.[8]

Saving for college is a long term effort, and most parents are small investors who suffer from a variety of problems. Small investors are usually unable to diversify their investments in such a way as to provide protection from changing market conditions. They usually lack both the time and expertise to manage their portfolio properly for this type of long term investment. Lastly, the need to manage long term investments through a number of market cycles is something most small investors cannot clearly see how to do.[9]

The Academic Bank may be a vehicle for families to use to accumulate capital for college savings, or for that matter for savings of any kind (within regulatory guidelines). By pooling together the relatively small investments of many families, a college or university may be able to provide an opportunity that otherwise would be beyond the reach, or beyond the understanding, of many individual investors. By thinking creatively, a college or university may be able to make savings a convenient and easy activity.

The target market for this type of college savings plan, surprisingly enough, is likely to be the faculty, staff, and perhaps alumni of a college or university, not future matriculants. As with college tuition prepayment programs, it is important not to allow participants in the program to feel that there is any implication that admissions policy is in any way affected by participation in a savings program (referred to as "implied admissions"). For this reason, and since savings for college is a long-term endeavor that needs to start well before the child is even in secondary school, it would be unwise to market a college-based savings program to potential matriculants specifically.

Aside from this, the faculty and staff of a college or university are a very captive market. Lack of convenience is one obstacle to regular savings, which is why U.S. Savings Bonds are such a popular form of savings for individuals and families. Most colleges and universities already provide payroll deduction for savings bonds, as well as for credit union deposits if a credit union exists on campus. Using this mechanism of convenience to further savings for college, and provide needed capital to satisfy institutional needs, should be relatively straightforward. One would also hope that the faculty and staff of an academic institution should understand the need to save for college, even with employee benefits which at best cover tuition and fees alone.

This suggests a change in typical employee benefits plans, and a careful examination of all relevant local, state and Federal regulations surrounding deposit acceptance and appropriate use of these funds. More questions than answers immediately come to mind: Would the savings be restricted for college use? What happens when an employee leaves the college or university? Can a participant petition for and receive early withdrawal of funds?

Allowing alumni to contribute is an even more interesting notion. They might be offered an opportunity to "invest" in their *alma mater*'s future by sharing a portion of the return on their investment with the college or university itself. All other things being equal, alumni may choose to invest with their *alma mater* just as many individuals choose their favorite charitable organization through which to arrange their credit card. Another interesting benefit may be some residual tax benefits to the donor if the college or university benefits from holding the investment. The amount of benefit could easily be a source of charitable contributions for alumni.

In order to properly provide for college savings, the Academic Bank will have to perform two banking functions. First, it will have to accept deposits in some convenient form. These deposits could be in the form of conventional (commercial/savings and loan) bank deposits, savings bank share purchases, or fund purchases of some kind. Deposit acceptance could be achieved through a mechanism of convenience, such as direct deduction from employee pay checks or direct, routine transfer from an external commercial bank account. Second, the Academic Bank will have to perform some kind of intermediation service to benefit the depositors. More than likely, what will be required is some kind of portfolio transformation to take the funds deposited by the participants and create a long term investment sufficient to generate an adequate level of income at an acceptable level of risk. The college or university will have to examine a number of factors in deciding how to make its investments, and will have to examine all of its goals in deciding whether to pass the benefits of any excess earnings (after operating expenses) completely back to the depositors, or share the benefits to further some other institutional goal.

A second function of the Academic Bank is that of *providing loans to students*. Loans have increased significantly over the past fifteen years as a proportion of total student aid, and income tests on Stafford loans (formerly GSL's) have made those even less attainable for students whose families are in certain income brackets. In general, the availability of government backed loans has not kept pace with the need for these loans, or financial aid in general. The growing gap between available financial aid and financial need has caused many institutions to try to bolster their institutional aid. The size of a college or university's financial aid endowment also affects its need for additional institutional loan sources.

The Academic Bank, at the college or university's choice, may be able to offer supplemental loans at different terms than Federally or state backed loans. For some institutions, there is a need to offer loans at more competitive interest rates than the market normally offers to students who do not qualify for Federal or state loans, or who do not qualify in sufficient quantity. For other colleges and universities, there is a need to offer loans that extend for a longer payoff period than the government loans. For yet others, an institutional loan program may be a feature of a tuition prepayment program or an alternative student expense financing program.

Loans may also be needed by a college or university for other purposes as well. At many institutions, loans are used for faculty/staff mortgages, or for swing loans for faculty, staff, and students who may be in need of short term credit. At still other institutions, loans are used administratively to provide funds to departments in advance of gift receipts, and to perform internal financing for departmental purchases or capital projects (this itself is a common use of bank-like functions). Each college or university will need to examine its institutional goals to determine which use of funds for loans it requires.

In order to be able to provide loans, the Academic Bank needs to provide certain intermediation services to its customers, namely brokerage services. In this context, the Academic Bank is merely arranging for the lenders and borrowers of capital to get together more conveniently than they may have been able to on their own. The college or university will typically reach an agreement with a lender to offer loans to an identified set of constituencies. The lender is supplying the funds, and the individual borrower is fully liable directly to the lender for repayment. The Academic Bank should, however, be able to exert its influence to achieve the best possible terms for its constituencies in return for a "captive market" for the lender. This captive market may provide a lower credit risk to the lender either by virtue of its characteristics (personal, educational) or merely its affiliation with the college or university. The captive market represents one or more of the potential loan recipients discussed just above.

A third closely related function of the Academic Bank is *funding loans*, distinctly different than just providing loans as in the previous section. In this case, the college or university chooses to be the actual lender to whom the borrower (student, faculty, or whomever) is liable. A college or university may choose to do this either to retain more control over the event, or because it chooses to itself bear the risk in order to reap the financial benefit (disintermediation). While the reasons for these loans may be the same as above, different banking functions and structures will allow the Academic Bank to fund loans with capital generated from the activities of the Academic Bank itself rather than merely make loans with existing, or external, sources of capital.

In order to fund student loans, the Academic Bank must accept some form of deposits in order to generate the necessary capital to lend. The mere lending of this capital to one of its constituencies is itself an act of intermediation. In this case, the Academic Bank is performing portfolio transformation. It is restructuring the original capital received in the form of deposits into a new type of instrument, a loan asset. The loans themselves may be held until repayment, or may be sold in a secondary market if possible. Depending on the institution, and the kinds of individuals to whom the loans have been made, these loans may be very attractive on the open market. Depending on the state in which the college or university resides, there may be opportunities created by loan guarantee agencies in the state to market these loans as well.

Yet another function of the Academic Bank is *funding financial aid grants* to the college or university's students. Unlike the goal of funding financial aid loans above, this involves using the Academic Bank to generate capital which can be provided to students with no pay back required. Obviously, this is the most attractive form of student aid from the student's point of view, and the most difficult for which to raise external funding from the college or university's point of view. Once again, many colleges and universities are substantially under-endowed, and even more severely under-endowed when it comes to financial aid dollars.

As in the case of funding loans, in order to fund grants the Academic Bank will need to raise substantial capital through some type of deposit. Transaction services may need to be offered in order to attract a larger set of depositors or investors. Since the grants are not going to bring in any revenue of their own at all, the demand for capital in this program is extreme. Once funds begin to accumulate, some substantial intermediation services will need to be provided. More than likely both brokerage and portfolio transformation will need to take place, with greater emphasis on portfolio transformation as a way to generate the needed revenue which can be made available to fund financial aid grants.

As will be shown in the next chapter, PMU projects a substantial deficit in its available institutional grant aid—over $11 million. The capital necessary to provide a return on investment to even approach this need annually would be several hundred million dollars (assuming a rate of return similar to that which PMU receives on its general endowment). Of course, a college or university need not take an "all or nothing" approach: even a modest accumulation of capital can play some part in providing a useful revenue stream for price discounting.

A fifth function of the Academic Bank is providing a vehicle through which a college or university can *provide a broad range of financial services* to one or more of its constituencies. These services may be provided for a variety of reasons: to achieve some administrative efficiency by streamlining financial services throughout the organization; as a marketing tool to offer students, faculty and/or staff a more complete and convenient academic environment; leveraging financial assets in different parts of the organization; improving relations with external financial entities; and others.

In order to provide these services, once again, the Academic Bank will need to accept deposits in some form. Deposits for students could be made by parents either at the beginning of a school year or semester, or periodically during the year. Student financial aid and student employment earnings could all be channeled into this deposit account creating a tightly coupled system. Faculty and staff could be offered some of the same benefits. The short term interest earnings generated by the accumulated funds may even provide sufficient resources to cover administrative expenses.

The Academic Bank will need to offer transaction services as well. These represent the desire on a college or university's part to minimize the number of steps a student, faculty or staff member has to do to perform a financial transaction on campus. A student or faculty/staff "account" can be used to perform transactions within campus, and with local merchants. In addition, a debit and/or credit card can be instituted to facilitate these transactions even more.

Finally, the Academic Bank will have to provide intermediation services, more than likely in the form of brokerage services, to complete the suite of broad services to be offered. In this way, funds deposited can be invested in some instrument if the depositor desires, or credit can be extended into the depositor's account, both through the services provided by the Academic Bank. In this way, the depositor is offered the ultimate in convenience, with the potential for the college or university to generate funds to satisfy some other goal.

A final function of the Academic Bank, perhaps a subset of providing broad financial services, is that of *providing a debit/credit card* for campus and near-campus financial transactions. A debit/credit card may be provided for student convenience as described above, or to reduce the potential for crimes against individuals by reducing the amount of cash being carried by students, faculty, and staff on campus. Encouraging a more cashless society has become an interesting mechanism to combat crime on urban campuses particularly. By working with local merchants, and offering them the option of accepting a campus debit card in exchange for very favorable or free transaction costs, cash reduction can be extended beyond the strict confines of a campus.

At minimum, the Academic Bank would have to offer transaction services to support the debit/credit card. If these transaction services would be performed through the use of a debit card, the Academic Bank would need to accept deposits of some kind to achieve positive balances to draw down as transactions are performed. If the transaction services would be performed through the use of a credit card, brokerage services would need to be performed to provide the needed credit for transactions. Hopefully, a large enough pool of depositors could provide sufficient reserves for the Academic Bank to extend credit using these funds to the customers who require it.

Academic Bank Functions and Banking Structures

Each of the functions of the Academic Bank can be satisfied by creating a bank emulating one or more of the pre-existing structures described in Figure 4.1 in the last chapter. This next section will examine the individual functions detailed above and the banking structures that may be used to satisfy them.

The first Academic Bank function is that of promoting *college savings*. Based on the required banking functions from Figure 5.2, two types of banking structures become most appropriate. First, mutual funds are extremely attractive. They provide an easy vehicle for investment which is convenient, flexible, and which usually provides a good return. Since mutual funds are not strictly depository, but involve share purchases, they are also outside of the regulatory jurisdiction of the banking industry. The Academic Bank could either create its own mutual funds (real portfolio transformation), or as a variation, simply funnel purchases to existing mutual funds in a way similar to the manner in which many colleges and universities provide access to a variety of funds for retirement benefit contributions (just brokerage services).

Some specialized college savings mutual funds have already been established, either as investment alternatives or as tuition prepayment alternatives. The College Savings Bank in Princeton, New Jersey has devised and patented savings devices whose rate of return adjusts with the change in the price of tuition at 500 top schools as measured by the College Board. The Canadian government's Registered Education Savings Plan is an example of a successful tax sheltered savings account insured by the Canadian government that earns a high rate of interest. There are quite a few state plans that have been mentioned as well.

Insurance companies offer yet another structure for college savings, perhaps one of the few remaining structures that allow for funds to accumulate tax free. One particularly attractive option is using a single premium life insurance policy. Under the Tax Reform Act of 1986 (as amended in 1988), parents may take out such a policy for a child, and providing they allow annual premiums to be paid into the policy for at least seven years, they may borrow the cash value and use it for educational costs without triggering a taxable event. This type of policy has a growing liquidation value prior to payment of the death benefit.[10]

In November, 1990 new Federal tax legislation increased the tax liabilities of insurance companies on many kinds of policies. Probably a direct outgrowth of the belief that insurance companies did not pay enough taxes, the legislation increased taxable income by increasing the period over which deductible expenses on policies must be amortized by the insurer. Undoubtedly, most insurers choose to pass the majority of this effective tax increase on to their policy holders.[11] This raises the costs to the Academic Bank that chooses to issue insurance policies to its customers. Another problem with investing for college through insurance is the high level of fees and commissions siphoned off by insurance agents, especially from early premium payments. Yet another problem is that although the earnings under many life insurance policies accumulate tax free, they are usually fully taxable when the money is withdrawn.[12]

Finally, as with mutual funds, the Academic Bank can either take on the properties of an insurance company and provide policies that have the desired characteristics (portfolio transformation), or it can serve as an intermediary and provide access to the appropriate insurance instruments for its constituencies (brokerage services).

While many, if not all, of the banking structures being discussed can and do *provide loans*, the only structure strictly speaking that exists only to finance loans is the consumer credit company. These non-bank banks have been competitors to other forms of banking for some time, offering convenience to their customers and easy access to credit typically for retail purchases. The funds for new loans become self-generating as the volume and payoff rates increase.

The Academic Bank solely interested in providing loans to one or more of its constituencies could easily pattern itself after a consumer credit company. As long as the college or university has a reserve of capital with which to seed the start-up of the company this is a viable option. Colleges and universities do have access to some unique capital markets, such as borrowing from Sallie Mae at extremely favorable rates of interest, which could be used as seed money. Within time, the payback from the initial loans will not only cover operating expenses, but will eventually allow future loans to be subsidized to achieve the best possible rates.

If *funding loans* was the only function of the Academic Bank a college or university needed to perform, either a mutual fund or insurance company structure would be most appropriate to satisfy this goal. Full-service institutions, such as commercial banks, savings and loans, mutual savings banks, and credit unions, can provide the services necessary to accomplish this goal, but not without offering many other non-essential services as well. Mutual funds and insurance companies are uniquely positioned to provide vehicles to accumulate capital and transform the capital into loan assets for the Academic Bank.

The mutual fund provides the most flexible way to allow many small investors to pool their savings in an easy and profitable way. If part of the asset holdings of the mutual fund were the loans that needed to be funded, and these loans provided a sufficiently attractive rate of return, this becomes a quite desirable alternative. Care would need to be taken to balance short term and long term assets held by the mutual fund, as well as to provide the necessary diversification to ensure fund stability.

Insurance provides an equally attractive way to accumulate funds tax-free for ultimate transformation into loan assets. Once again, care must be taken to provide sufficient reserves for death benefits that may need to be paid out. It may also be desirable to limit the number of policies against which loans may be taken by the policy holder since this activity will limit the funds available for loans to other constituencies by the Academic Bank itself.

Funding grants requires the largest generation of capital, and the most extensive intermediation services possible in order to generate the largest return to be distributed as financial aid grants. While many banking structures can provide the necessary resources and services, the commercial bank stands out as the best. It tries to cultivate the biggest customers, provides the most extensive and diverse services, and has ties to virtually every other type of financial services institution. A college or university should not rule out owning and operating a commercial bank, even if it is ruled by the IRS to be a taxable enterprise. The potential for reasonable levels of revenue may outweigh the unfamiliar bite of taxes.

The fifth function is *providing broad financial services*. Since the goal here is comprehensiveness, and not necessarily revenue generation, any number of banking structures can perform the task. Once again, commercial banks, savings and loans, mutual savings banks, and credit unions can all provide the necessary services. It is likely, however, that unlike the goal of funding financial aid grants, commercial banks are least likely to be the best choice because of the complexity, tax, and regulatory implications that come along with a college or university buying or establishing a commercial bank. Also, the client base is more likely to be the individual student, staff member and/or faculty member, making a savings and loan or mutual savings bank structure more appropriate. These types of institutions are better at providing smaller transactions in a more personable way to small depositors or investors.

Many colleges or universities may find that they already have Federal credit unions existing on campus. These associations, usually founded by faculty and staff together or separate from students, usually provide limited transaction services. They exist primarily to provide easy savings, often through payroll deduction, and primarily to provide consumer loans to their members after a period of time making deposits. As a result of deregulation, credit unions can offer a wide variety of services that may make them a good target for expansion at a college or university that wishes to provide broader financial services.

Finally, more and more colleges and universities are evaluating and *providing a debit and/or credit card* for campus use by students and/or faculty and staff for reasons of convenience and/or security. Duke University has implemented a card that not only provides a single instrument of identification for its students, but provides access to two prepaid expense accounts, one for dining services at any one of eighteen on-campus facilities and the campus general store, and one for flexible spending at one of six university stores.[13]

Once again, commercial banks, savings and loans, mutual savings banks, and credit unions can all provide the necessary services. But, most of them are also likely to provide more than enough services, including some unnecessary ones. Also, depending on whether both credit and debit services will be offered, one or more of these full-service institutions may be better. If credit services are involved, the

Academic Bank must be able to offer the necessary credit, and therefore must be able to generate sufficient capital to have funds to lend. This may require offering some ancillary services in addition to the debit/credit card.

Some Final Observations

As with any other financial undertaking, in order for a college or university to start an Academic Bank it must prepare a business plan outlining the goals to be satisfied, the functions that need to be performed, and the markets that need to be targeted. While the framework discussed here assumes that a single college or university would work on its own, it is possible for a consortium approach to be used. While a single-school project both ensures some competitive advantage with respect to peer institutions, as well as allows the strength of a college or university's reputation to help market its "products," a consortium provides the advantages of cooperation based on either a geographic region or institution type. While a consortium approach reduces any competitive advantage within its member schools, it strengthens competitive advantage with institutions outside of the consortium. A group of schools may also collectively enhance the reputation of the Academic Bank. Another advantage of a consortium is the likelihood that no single school will carry a large enough portion of the liability to affect its financial statements. A consortium made up of nominally competing schools would make the Internal Revenue Service more than likely view any revenue generated by the Academic Bank as non-taxable income for the Bank, rather than as unrelated (taxable) business income for the non-profit member schools.

If a consortium approach is chosen, a strategy would have to be developed for choosing the member schools, and for picking the board of trustees. The member schools would need to all benefit in some way from the enterprise, though not necessarily share the same institutional goals. It might be helpful if all the schools were in the same geographical region to assist in marketing and development of the Academic Bank. The board of trustees would need to be composed primarily of impartial members without any vested interest in any particular member schools.

Notes

1. Anderson (1990), pp. 7-8.
2. Muffett, *et. al*, p. 3.
3. *Ibid.*, p. 18.
4. Natala K. Hart, "How Families Are Saving for College: What Market Surveys Tell Us." in *College Savings Plans: Public Policy Choices.* Janet S. Hansen, ed. (New York: The College Board, 1990), p. 42.
5. "Save, America: A Primer on U.S. Savings and Its Effect on Economic Health," p. 13.
6. "Counting on Savings," editorial, *Wall Street Journal* (19 January 1990), p. A10.
7. Institute for Research on the Economics of Taxation, p. 4.
8. Sandy Baum, "The Need for College Savings," in *College Savings Plans: Public Policy Choices.* Janet S. Hansen, ed. (New York: The College Board, 1990), p. 12.
9. Anderson (1989b), pp. 5—6.
10. Nancy G. McDuff, "Financing the Costs of Higher Education: Planning Creative Student and Institutional Options," *Planning for Higher Education* 18(1), (Ann Arbor, MI: Society for College and University Planning, 1989), pp. 29-30.
11. Susan Pulliam, "Life Insurance Firms Plan to Pass Along Big Tax Increases to their Policyholders," *Wall Street Journal* (10 December 1990), p. A7A.
12. Ellen E. Shultz, "College Savings Plans That May Not Make the Grade," *Wall Street Journal* (4 November 1991), p. C1.
13. Wes Newman and Boll Ignelzi, "Selecting a Campus-Wide Card System" (Durham, N.C.: Duke University, 1990), n.p.

VI
Case Study: The Academic Bank at PMU

Introduction

The first section of this study (Chapters 1, 2 and 3) focused on the key challenges facing higher education in the area of affordability and student financing. It began with a discussion of the causes of escalating costs in higher education, and their effect on the price of attendance. Next, the concepts of price discounting and net price of attendance were introduced. A model was developed to suggest ways for individual institutions to understand the degree to which their students are sensitive to the net price of attendance, and the model was tested by examining data from three schools of different types.

The second section of the study (Chapters 4 and 5) focused on a potential solution to some of the challenges raised in the first section. Both the structure and function of banking institutions in the United States were reviewed, with a broad definition of "bank" being employed. The schema developed from this review was then used to describe the potential look of an Academic Bank.

This final chapter will apply the concepts of the Academic Bank in one sample institutional context to suggest strategies for this institution to solve some of its problems in student financing. This case study will involve PMU, the private multiversity from Chapter 3. PMU represents the most expensive and complex of those involved in this study, and in many ways the one that is already the most sophisticated in its approach to student financing issues.

Method of Analysis

Interviews were conducted with a wide range of administrators at PMU as a basis for understanding the specific challenges faced by the institution, and as a way to elicit ideas and suggestions. The individuals interviewed are listed in Table 6.1.

Provost
Deputy Provost
Executive Vice President
Acting Vice President for Human Resources
Treasurer
Associate Treasurer
Assistant Vice President for Policy Planning
Director, Communications
Director, Institutional Research
Development
    Vice President
    Director, Planned Giving
    Director, Alumni Relations
Student Financial Services
    Associate Vice President
    Director, Product Development & Marketing
    Director, Student Financial Aid
Director, ID Center
Associate Dean, business school
Associate Professor, Regional Sciences Department

Table 6.1 - Interview List for PMU Case Study

Interviews were conducted over several months. Most conversations were only semi-structured resulting in the majority of the questions being addressed through general conversation. A summary document discussing the basic ideas behind the Academic Bank was provided to each interview subject in advance. In addition to the interviews, official publications of the university and relevant internal reports were available for examination.

Results

The interviews at PMU focused on three aspects of the Academic Bank: issues of necessity, whether there was sufficient need to consider creating an Academic Bank, including issues of price sensitivity; issues of appropriateness, the opinions of the interview subjects about whether an Academic Bank seemed proper for the institution; and issues of feasibility, whether some form of Academic Bank could be created at PMU.

Necessity

The first area explored was the necessity of implementing additional bank-like functions at PMU. At best, PMU officials felt that middle class families only save what is necessary for the equivalent of a public education. Parents fund more of college education through current cash flow and less through savings. PMU officials felt the need to develop the institution's relationship with the matriculant and family and provide programs to help them manage this critical point in their financial lives, the in-school and immediate post-school years.

Since price sensitivity has been observed at PMU most among the least aided students, middle class families who fall into this category may feel that the price of PMU is out of reach. These families may be unwilling to adjust their lifestyle sufficiently to use current income dollars to supplement their savings for college, and may feel no choice but to send their children to less expensive (likely public) institutions.

The current system of broad-based financing (*i.e.* Stafford Loan Program) is not helping these price sensitive families. PMU recognized the need for a replacement system that would enhance the resources that students and their families have to use to pay for college. As indicated in Chapter 1, an increasing share of traditional price discounting, need-based financial aid, is being awarded in the form of loans. Many students and families view the burden of repayment as an undue hardship in the immediate post-college years. Additionally, there is concern that such programs as the Stafford Loan program create too large a liability for the government due to the interest rate subsidy (and increasing default rates) in the recession and post-recession period.

While reducing the self-help component may have been attractive to students and their families, officials at PMU recognized the need to develop new mechanisms to limit the dependence on its own inadequate unrestricted financial aid dollars. To do this, PMU felt that new sources of loan and grant funds must be discovered or developed. Among the unique challenges PMU identified were:

- A significant financial aid shortfall for aided students (let alone unaided) in the next five years.
- Severe limits in restricted aid dollars compared to its peers.

- A greater self-help component to its aid packages than its peers.
- Extremely limited institutional loan funds available.

PMU projected a severe shortfall in the coming few years in the funds available to discount the price of attendance through institutionally-funded financial aid. The Office of Institutional Research at PMU prepared a five-year projection model of financial aid income and expenditure, using 1991-92 as the base year for calculations. The initial summary is displayed in Table 6.2 (note that the surplus/deficit is annual, not cumulative across the years).

		Year1	Year2	Year3	Year4	Year5
Financial Aid	Unrest Budget	$30,142,264	$30,142,264	$30,142,264	$30,142,264	$30,142,264
	Unrest Budget Need	$30,056,438	$32,486,027	$35,156,331	$37,866,651	$41,056,135
	Surplus (Deficit)	$85,826	($2,343,763)	($5,014,067)	($7,724,387)	($10,913,871)

Table 6.2 - Financial Aid Summary for PMU

The model projected an annual shortfall of institutional financial aid dollars of over $10.9 million by the end of the fifth year. When the model was enhanced to enforce limits on Stafford loans year by year, the projected shortfall grew to over $11.4 million (see Table 6.3).

		Year1	Year2	Year3	Year4	Year5
Financial Aid	Unrest Budget	$30,142,264	$30,142,264	$30,142,264	$30,142,264	$30,142,264
	Unrest Budget Need	$30,056,438	$32,486,027	$35,156,331	$37,903,971	$41,576,411
	Surplus (Deficit)	$85,826	($2,343,763)	($5,014,067)	($7,761,707)	($11,434,147)

Table 6.3 - Enhanced Financial Aid Summary for PMU

A study examining financial aid for the 1990-91 academic year showed that while only 6% of institutional grant aid at PMU came from restricted sources (fundraising and endowment) its ten top competitors averaged 43% of their institutional aid from these sources! Individual schools ranged from 21% to 93%.

PMU noticed that while the use of self-help as a price discount mechanism was less attractive to a prospective student than an outright grant, students with higher self-help components had fewer competitive offers from other colleges or universities. With the elimination of the Overlap group (of which PMU was a member), however, differences in self-help will likely become more significant as the aid policies of these competing institutions drift apart and become more and more heterogeneous. PMU might expect to see more price sensitivity emerge in the future due to these differences in self-help awards.

Officials at PMU were also concerned about their ability to maintain need blind admissions. In July 1992 PMU's University Council Committee on Undergraduate Admissions and Financial Aid issued a report on the university's need-blind admissions policy. Among its conclusions the committee recommended that

1. The current need-blind admissions policy is essential in recruiting and maintaining a diverse and talented student body.
2. The University administration is urged to explore other means of addressing projected budgetary shortfalls before taking what appears to be the irreversible step of altering our present need-blind admissions policy.
3. The University should aim for a long-term goal of generating $150 million of endowment for undergraduate financial aid within the next five years.[1]

If PMU is committed to need-blind admissions, as well as cultural and ethnic diversity, it will need to take steps to ensure that it has sufficient aid and alternatives available to ensure the continuation of these policies.

Another source of concern was PMU's ability to attract and retain foreign students, who are not eligible for government sponsored financial aid. Accomplishing this goal is also dependent upon PMU's ability to generate new sources of financial assistance. PMU continues to strive for ethnic and cultural diversity, as well as recognize its role in providing educational opportunities to students from other countries. It has cultivated significant ties to the educational and business worlds in the Pacific rim, South Asia (Indian subcontinent), Middle East, and Europe. These students are often funded by their respective governments only for a year at a time, occasionally producing sudden financial hardship when students lose their sponsors midway through their program. Similarly, PMU's ability to collect delinquent funds is hard enough within the United States and nearly impossible overseas.

All of these issues highlight the need for educational financing for college to be understood as one component of a personal financing life cycle. An adult typically faces four high-cost financial needs: purchase of a house, college financing for one's children, retirement, and dependent care for the elderly. Into this one often brings the financial burden of one's own college education. The prospect of additional lifelong education is ever-growing. These four major cost items are all long-term capital needs that need to be planned for and financed as a set of lifelong financial objectives.

Parents are often ill-equipped to make the timely decisions necessary to provide for these four (or five) major needs, let alone the unexpected problems caused by extended illness or unemployment. PMU needs to find ways to assist parents of current and prospective matriculants in planning for these eventualities. The goal is to be sure that the net price to students and their families is acceptable both in the in-school as well as post-graduation years, and that students and their families do not make the mistake of avoiding PMU due to "sticker shock."

At the same time, PMU officials recognize the need to reduce the cost of attendance through all possible means. To do so, they must focus on cost reduction in the academic enterprise in addition to focusing on price discounts. While even with the best intentions of eliminating "cost plus" pricing, PMU cannot escape quickly from the fact that nearly a third of its revenue (excluding health services revenue from its affiliated medical center) comes from tuition. The administrators recognize that they need to make the academic enterprise more efficient. PMU is currently attempting to reduce the administrative component of the institution by 15% over five years through a variety of quality management and administrative process re-engineering programs. The savings from these steps are to be captured and diverted to instruction and research. Similar programs are being piloted in some schools and departments and directly targeted to the efficiency of instruction and research.

There was concern on the part of some interviewees that PMU may not be sufficiently innovative to respond to these needs quickly. There may therefore be a role for certain colleges and universities to facilitate the entrance of others into this arena either by coordinating partnerships or consortia, or providing needed services for a fee. While there is potential in alliances and joint ventures with other institutions, these options remain out of the scope of this study. Of course, when considering options that have the potential to raise revenue from outside sources, it is necessary to be sensitive to the potential for PMU to jeopardize its tax exempt status by generating "unrelated business income," unrelated, that is, to the primary educational mission of the institution.

Appropriateness

Next, issues of appropriateness were explored. It is clear that the real financial needs discussed above compel PMU to at least consider some action. Administrators at PMU felt uniformly that the needs they outlined left PMU with little choice but to pursue new options in this area and implement them if at all feasible. PMU is a complex financial institution already. Many bank-like functions are already taking place; adding others should be consistent with a pattern of service offerings that has developed over a number of years.

Following the model of academic bank functions discussed in Chapter 5, Table 6.4 displays these current activities. Items appearing in *italics* are of particular significance and will be discussed more fully below. PMU provides functions and services in every category of the academic bank model. These services involve multiple constituencies (students, faculty, staff, and even alumni), and relationships to various independent financial services organizations (*e.g.* commercial banks for loan origination, federal funds clearinghouse for payroll direct deposit, commercial clearinghouse for credit card transaction processing).

Three of these functions linked closely to financial aid are of particular significance.

Student billing account

As with most universities, PMU bills students and their families for most costs related to attendance through a student account. This account functions as a credit account: the student receives periodic statements as charges are incurred, and is given a period of time within which to pay. Late fees are assessed and collected on outstanding balances remaining past the due date. Charges typically include tuition and fees, on-campus residential living including dining services, library fines, additional department or school related fees, and monthly telephone charges for residential students (PMU maintains and administers its own PBX). Similarly, financial aid awards are directly credited against the student account (grants and loans, internal and external). A student's ability to graduate or have a transcript released by the university can be withheld if the student is not in good financial standing.

> College Savings
>   Student and/or employee credit union
>   U.S. Savings Bond purchase through payroll deduction
> Provide Loans
>   *Student loans for financial aid (GSL*, NDSL, etc.)
>   Faculty/staff/student swing loans
>   Faculty/staff mortgage guarantee program
> Fund Loans
>   Student loans for financial aid
>   *Tuition prepayment plan*
>   Departmental loans in advance of gifts
>   Intra-university loans for capital goods acquisition
> Fund grants
>   Institutional grants for financial aid
> Provide broad financial services
>   Check cashing services
>   Institution sponsored travel cards (American Express)
>   Student receivables processing
>   Lock box services
>   Wire transfers
>   Cashiering services
>   Payroll direct deposit
>   Campus automated teller machines
>   Trust services
> Provide debit and/or credit card services
>   *Student billing account*
>   Institution sponsored credit cards
>   Credit card merchant processing

Table 6.4 - Current Bank-like Functions at PMU

Many other miscellaneous fees are often collected through the student account. By and large these charges need to be closely tied to the teaching or housing of students. The student is presented with a single unified bill. Partial payments received by the university require distribution back to the various possible service providers who fed their

Case Study: The Academic Bank at PMU

charges to the student account. A carefully negotiated "pecking order" exists to decide which organization receives its reimbursement first. While there is pressure to bill more and more through the student account to reduce administrative overhead and leverage central billing even more, this is balanced by the reality that the larger service providers (like the schools who charge tuition and fees, and residential living which provides housing) will usually get their money first, leaving other service providers to scurry and try to collect their smaller fees.

Tuition prepayment/long-term financing plans

For almost ten years PMU has had a very successful tuition prepayment plan. Actually, a whole suite of plans has been developed and offered first to undergraduates, then to some graduate/professional students. The first plan is a tuition prepayment plan which allows students to prepay all four years of tuition upon initial matriculation and be shielded from likely tuition increases in subsequent years. For those students who cannot afford to make the up-front payment in cash, a fixed rate loan (ten year maximum pay back period) is secured through a participating commercial bank. The bank uses funds secured by a large certificate of deposit held by the university to make the loans.

A second program provides a simple line of credit which can be drawn upon by qualifying students and their families to pay for almost any educational expense at PMU. Interest on the loan, which can be secured through home equity, is usually prime rate plus 1%, and can be combined with a prepayment plan loan at the same rate. A third program is an interest free monthly budgeting plan for charges that are billed to the student account.

All three of these programs were instituted to assist students and their families to better afford the price of attendance at PMU. The first program actually freezes the net price of attendance at the price of the first year. While there were no data in Chapter 3 to evaluate the price sensitivity of full-pay students, their use of this program may be one indicator since it allows students and their families to limit the growth in price. If credit is required, the ten-year financing allows a family to reduce the out-of-pocket expenses year by year (while incurring a long-term liability, of course). Alternatively, the ten-year financing allows a family the option of passing the burden of payment on to the student after graduation. The second and third programs, lines of credit and monthly budgeting, do little to control the net price of attendance, but do provide easy to use credit mechanisms to help pay for college.

Figure 6.1 shows the new dollars spent through the prepayment programs (cash and loan) over their first nine years. Figure 6.2 shows the number of participants.

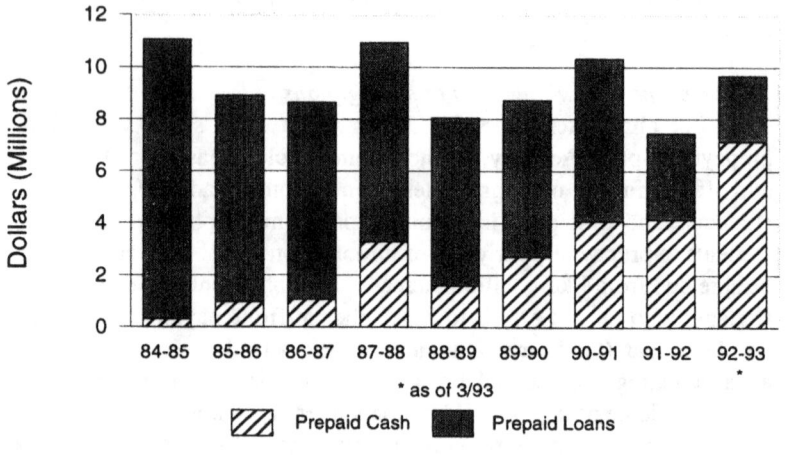

Figure 6.1 - PMU Prepayment Plans: New Dollars

Overall volume of dollars has fluctuated somewhat. Full cash participation (in dollars) increased steadily during the years, leveled off around the $4 million mark, then has surged in the current year to over $7 million. The prepaid loan program (in dollars) peaked during the first year that the plan was offered, leveled off at around the $6 million mark, then continued to drop quickly in the past two years. The number of new (as opposed to ongoing) participants in each plan largely mirrors the pattern of dollars. Participation in the cash plan has increased since its initial year of offering, and after steadying off has surged in the last year. The number of new participants in the loan plan has steadily decreased each year since its large peak when first offered.

Case Study: The Academic Bank at PMU 125

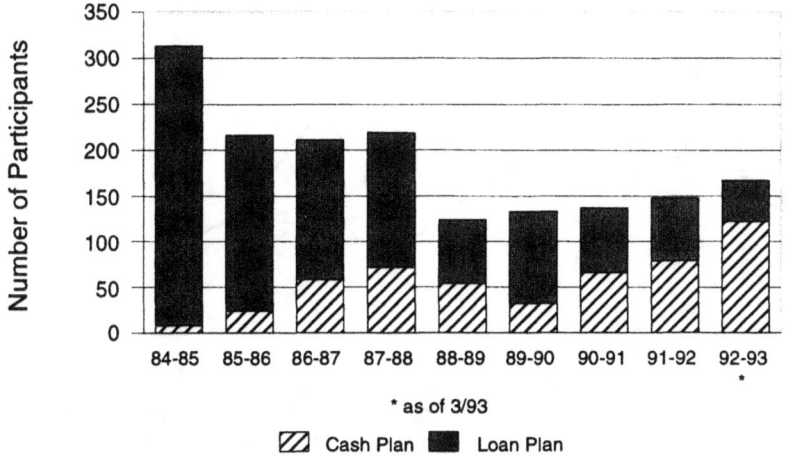

Figure 6.2 - PMU Prepayment Plans: New Participants

This shift from the loan program to the cash program was initially surprising. One might have expected participation in both plans to increase steadily. Several explanations are likely. The plans were initially offered at the height of high tuition increases of the 1980's. Figure 6.3 shows the change in the rate of increase in tuition and fees, at PMU during the same years for which there is data for the prepayment programs. Participation in the prepayment loan program (from Figure 6.2) fell dramatically as the rate of increase in tuition slowed from 1984 to 1987. New participation fell to one of its smallest levels in 1988 even though the change in price rebounded back to over 8.6%. After a slight increase in 1989, participation in the loan program continued to drop as the change in price dropped through 1992.

Chapter 3 provides data on the differences in yield for PMU for different classifications of students based on need and aid (Figure 3.4).

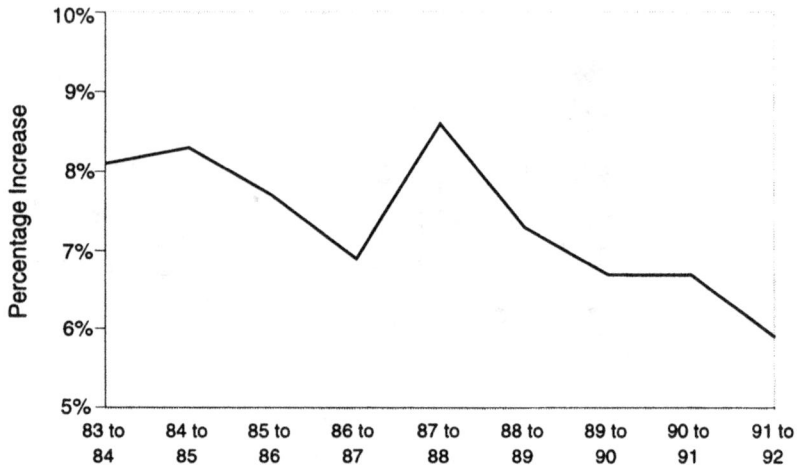

Figure 6.3 - Increase in Price of Tuition and Fees at PMU

There is a slight downward trend in the yield of students who applied for but did not receive need-based aid. A reduction in the matriculation of these students accounts for some of the fluctuation in the participation in the loan program. Because these students applied for financial aid but did not receive it, they would likely opt to use a prepayment plan given their lack of sufficient funds for cash prepayment (data was unavailable to verify this hypothesis).

Participation in the loan program has diminished more than PMU expected. Participation in the cash prepayment program has grown significantly more than PMU expected, especially in the past three years. Figure 6.2 shows an overall increase in number of participants since 1988-89, and this shifting from the loan to the cash program. The loan program retained its 10% fixed rate even through 1992-93. As interest rates in the marketplace continued to plunge during the early 1990's, more families financed their prepayment through cheaper, equity-based loans outside of the program. This accounted for much of the migration from the loan to the cash prepayment program. PMU expects to reverse this trend by reducing its interest rate on prepayment loans to 8.5% in 1993-94.

Case Study: The Academic Bank at PMU 127

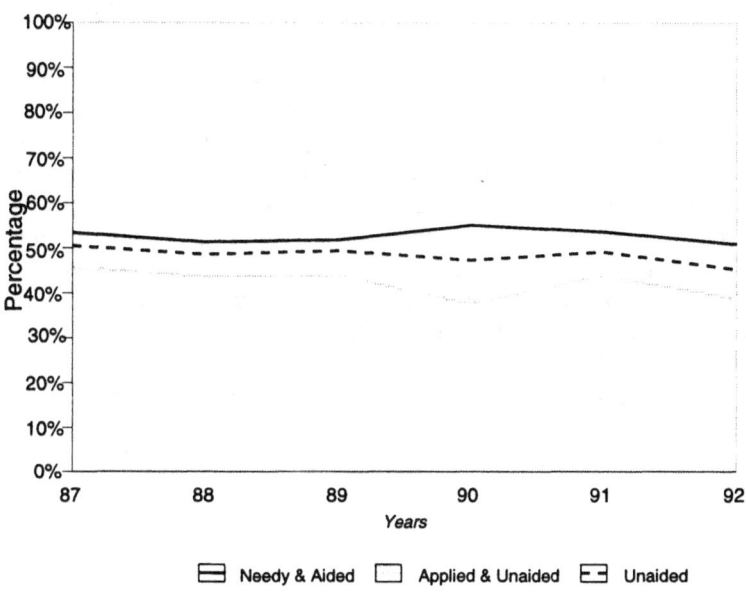

Figure 6.4 - Differences in Yield Percentage at PMU

Prepayment plans successfully lower the net price of attendance over the four years of matriculation. They have proven to be an attractive option, whether parents can afford the price outright (cash plan), or need to finance the prepayment amount (loan plan, or external financing). The data shadow the price sensitivity of the program participants. As the rate of increase in price eased in the late 1980's, the data show an easing of participation in these plans. As borrowing became more attractive with the single-digit interest rates of the early 1990's, participation seems to be picking up again as parents look for new ways to reduce the price of attendance and its impact on their household budget.

Student Loans for Financial Aid

PMU provides and facilitates many different kinds of loans for financial aid, especially with self-help representing an ever-increasing proportion of student aid awards. Various government subsidized loan programs are administered, including Perkins (formerly NDSL) and Stafford (formerly GSL) loans. One particular aspect of Stafford loan offering is worth special attention.

In the state in which PMU is located, many Stafford loans are issued and/or owned by the state loan guarantee agency (created by state statute and exempt from the state's simple but limiting usury law). PMU negotiated an arrangement whereby it would buy from the guarantee agency any Stafford loans that the agency had issued to its matriculated students and hold them during the period of time during which the students are enrolled. PMU receives the federal interest rate subsidy during these years. When the students leave PMU, the loans are bought back by the state guarantee agency which then bears any risk of collection or bad debt.

Figure 6.5 shows the level of Stafford Loans taken by PMU's students, and the amount of those loans purchased in turn by PMU. The proportion has increased dramatically (even with 1991-92 figures not being finalized).

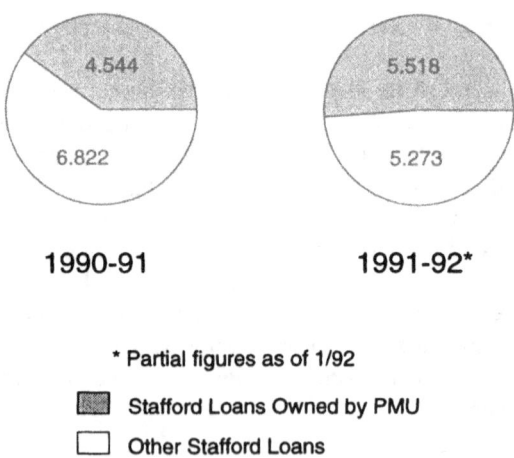

* Partial figures as of 1/92

▪ Stafford Loans Owned by PMU
☐ Other Stafford Loans

Figure 6.5 - Stafford Loan Amounts at PMU (millions of dollars)

Figure 6.6 shows the number of loans corresponding to the amounts in Figure 6.5. Once again, the proportion of loans purchased by PMU is increasing.

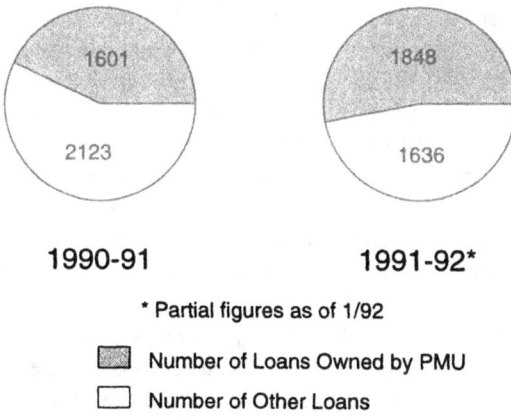

1990-91   1991-92*

* Partial figures as of 1/92

▨ Number of Loans Owned by PMU
☐ Number of Other Loans

Figure 6.6 - Number of Stafford Loan Borrows at PMU

Given the current use of bank-like activities at PMU, and the opinions of its senior administrators, it seems appropriate for PMU to continue to investigate creative ways for it to meet its financial needs. Commercial banking entities have failed to provide the mechanisms needed to satisfy the overall needs of students and their families. They are in the marketplace to make money, not to service students or their families.

The competitiveness of the banking industry has been very beneficial to its customers. Banks have continued to look for new ways to provide services, while at the same time collecting new fees. Nowhere has it proven to be more protective of its position in the marketplace than with respect to student loans. Commercial banks have profited well from the interest rate subsidy that the government has offered them on Stafford Loans. PMU has capitalized on this very same subsidy by disintermediating banks and retaining the premium for itself

(Figures 6.5 and 6.6). Banks have strongly resisted the current moves towards direct lending to students by educational institutions as an encroachment on their territory, whether it would be in the students' best interests or not. While readily reaping the benefits, the banking industry has done nothing creative in terms of understanding the problems and challenges that families with children in college face, or rising to the challenge of trying to solve those problems.

PMU senior management felt that anything that can be done to further the academic mission of PMU should be examined, tested, and implemented if sensible. Nothing should be ruled out without thorough analysis. Colleges and universities are already fairly commercialized. This is a necessary by-product of running a complex enterprise in the 1990's. PMU felt that it should not hesitate to be innovative for fear of being pinned with a commercialized label. On the other hand, no endeavor should be attempted without exploring fully the implications into the tax exempt status of the organization, or the full legal, regulatory, and political implications of any action. PMU's urban campus is virtually a city within a city: many commercial entities already exist on campus to service the diverse financial needs of its students, faculty and staff. Extending those services in new and different ways should be natural.

Especially in the area of student financing, it may be appropriate to offer assistance through a bank-like entity to reduce the anxiety of aid as "charity," of the "haves" helping the "have-nots." Banking is considered a "professional" activity. Casting financial assistance to students and their families in this context may have a positive residual benefit. Making ends meet may no longer be an act of charity on behalf of PMU, but rather a professionally counseled activity tailored to a family's specific needs.

Feasibility

Finally, issues of feasibility were identified. Colleges and universities bring a unique understanding of what parents and students go through and need during college years that banks do not generally possess. They can leverage this knowledge, and the relationship they already have with the student and family, to enhance the resources that students and their families have to use to pay for college by developing unique products to meet these needs.

Case Study: The Academic Bank at PMU

Colleges and universities possess two unique perspectives with respect to student financing. First, they have a long history of assisting families in dealing with issues of college affordability. Second, they possess a great deal of knowledge about the specific financial situations of students and their families, especially those students who apply for financial assistance. Most commercial financial institutions do not have nearly the quantity and quality of detailed financial information about a target market for financial services. These data not only could assist colleges and universities in tailoring specific programs aimed at the problems of specific types of students and their families, but the aggregate data provide important information about the state of the entire market for student financial services.

PMU must have new capital in order to continue to disintermediate banks and provide more student financial services on its own. The climate for fund raising for financial aid dollars is better than it has been in the past. Given the degree to which the middle class and even upper middle class have resorted to some form of financial assistance in the past fifteen years to afford college, financial aid is no longer perceived by the predominantly white middle and upper middle class simply as a mechanism for achieving "ethnic diversity." On the other hand, fundraising for financial aid at PMU has historically been tough enough that even an increase of several hundred percent would have only a limited impact. Nonetheless, PMU's goal is to raise $125 million of new financial aid endowment over the five years of its current capital campaign which will provide (when ultimately received) $6.25 million of annual revenues for undergraduate financial aid. An additional $5 million in term funds is being sought as well.

Another source of funds explored was accumulated savings. Savings programs could have a role to play with respect to a college or university's faculty and staff, as well as alumni. Many different savings and investment options are possible, as discussed in Chapters 4 and 5. Administrators believe that college savings programs will probably not be the most important activity of the Academic Bank at PMU. The more sophisticated the faculty at an institution (like PMU) the less likely that savings instruments developed by the college or university will be appealing compared to the diversity of options available in the commercial world. There are also significant regulatory implications to PMU becoming a depository of any kind. Some interesting ideas were discussed around the notion of using proceeds from an investment account that benefit the college or university as a charitable donation on behalf of an investor who agrees to allow part or all of the income to be given to the institution.

A comprehensive set of services offered by the Academic Bank may be the only way of ensuring sufficient protection from the risk associated with some of its activities. Outright purchase of a "real" bank may achieve the same ends with less incremental administrative effort. A major factor in any financial services activity is the risk involved—risk to the service provider and risk to the customer. Service providers go to extreme lengths to inform their customers about the risks involved in their decisions and choices. For PMU, and any college or university, simply "informing" a constituency about potential risk may not be sufficient. PMU would likely only provide services to individuals with some prior relationship to the university. Financial services offered by PMU must not be allowed to jeopardize this relationship.

PMU, therefore, has primary responsibility to minimize this risk. One major way to protect against financial risk is by sheer size of an operation. If a set of financial services is large enough (usually measured in dollars, number of participants, and diversity of offerings), excess funds in some areas are better able to balance shortages in others.

PMU must also be sensitive to its relationships with closely-linked financial services entities which are not directly a part of the university. PMU currently has two Federal credit unions, one for students and one for faculty and staff. These banking entities with close ties to the university (though clearly separate from it) could be important building blocks in developing the Academic Bank and PMU.

The student credit union, one of the largest in the country, currently services over 4,000 students for whom it functions as the primary retail banking institution. The employee credit union serves fewer individuals, most of whom use its services to qualify for low-interest consumer loans. Funds from these institutions may be accessible as seed capital through careful negotiations. PMU feels a responsibility not to undermine the viability of either of these institutions through competitive ventures. On the other hand, PMU does not feel it necessarily needs to enrich these entities either. Mutual cooperation will likely produce a win-win scenario, one in which the credit unions maintain their customers and service offerings, and PMU is able to provide additional complimentary services with the credit unions' cooperation.

The credit unions are not the only potential sources of seed capital. PMU has two potential additional sources of seed capital available to develop into the Academic Bank:

- Approximately $500,000 to $750,000 of institutional funds are available every year for a revolving loan program for students. These funds could be leveraged differently if necessary.
- PMU has the structures and willingness to develop innovative programs and capitalize their start-up costs so long as the programs at least break even over a defined number of years.

The institutional funds available to PMU for use as student loans are meager at best, less than 5% of the total loan activity of its undergraduates. These funds could perhaps be more productively used in other ways. Similarly, PMU has sufficient funds available in its own internal financing program to capitalize the start up of a new venture as long as its senior management is convinced of the ultimate self-sufficiency of the program after a pre-defined start-up period. This provides PMU with some degree of flexibility in initiating new programs.

Extending The Academic Bank at PMU: "Parental Partnership" Program[2]

It is clear that PMU already has the makings of an Academic Bank based on the activities it already pursues, especially in the area of student financial services. PMU's competitive advantage will be in building on its initial success to gain the confidence it needs to develop new programs. Banking can aggregate enough resources and programs to reduce the instability and volatility of student financing and provide the flexibility for PMU to solve some of its short-term and long-term problems.

The biggest student financing issue facing PMU is a large projected deficit in its available institutional grant dollars in the coming years (see Table 6.3). While the environment for fund raising for financial aid dollars is better than it ever was, the prospect of raising enough funds to significantly offset this projected shortfall is not encouraging. Other sources of capital are likely to be insufficient as well.

Aided students at the *lower* end of the need/aid spectrum show the most price sensitivity at PMU; however students with the *most* self-help would likely matriculate at PMU in significant numbers, since they are less likely to have better offers elsewhere (see Chapter 3). While the level of self help (albeit in a counter-intuitive way) may be a determining factor in a student's decision to matriculate, it may in fact be parental contribution that is as important a determining factor. The prepayment programs discussed above certainly are aimed at helping families manage and minimize parental contribution, though in most cases the parents using prepayment plans are contributing 100% of the price of attendance. Remember that parental contribution has two components: funds come from accumulated savings and investment, but even more commonly funds come from current earnings due to insufficient savings.

PMU needs to find a strategy to provide sufficient aid for the most needy to maintain need blind admissions, while at the same time ease the burden of parental contribution for the less needy, price sensitive families without scaring them away. All this must be accomplished in a framework of reducing availability of unrestricted financial aid dollars.

To accomplish these goals, rather than distribute aid packages from all the various sources (federal, state and institutional) as need-based aid according to a strict set of guidelines, PMU could reserve this precious aid for the most needy *only*. PMU could then meet the needs of the rest of the matriculants by focusing on its relationship with the parents, not the students. A program could be developed to make it as easy as possible for the parents of these lower need students to afford *their* portion of PMU's price—the parental contribution. A program not unlike the existing prepayment financing program could be implemented that allows parental contribution to be paid off over a long period of time (say, ten years). Any additional need would be met by additional self-help for the student.

Case Study: The Academic Bank at PMU

The actual data for PMU for 1992 (corresponding to Year 2 in the projections done in Table 6.3) show that for the lowest-need students (first 10% of population based on need, that is the first 389 of 3889 aided matriculating students), the vast majority of their aid is self help (first line in Table 6.5). They receive few grants, no SEOG allocation, and almost no institutional loans. By eliminating their conventional institutional aid (loans and grants) there would be little funding to spread to more needy students.

	Number of Students	Parental Contribution	Institutional Loans	Institutional Grants	SEOG	Total Self help	Total Grant	Total Aid
10% of Population by Need	389	$6,344,112	$18,720	$101,155	$0	$1,607,398	$349,826	$1,957,224
20% of Population by Need	778	$11,065,030	$56,784	$1,187,817	$11,980	$3,784,256	$1,739,717	$5,523,973
Break even with Projected Shortfall	1011	$13,334,090	$70,484	*$2,341,813*	$56,330	$5,060,387	$3,123,641	$8,184,028
30% of Population by Need	1167	$14,835,855	$88,159	$3,265,288	$78,230	$5,974,873	$4,181,329	$10,156,202

Table 6.5 - Aggregate Aid Levels for Segments of the Aided Population of PMU, 1992

At what point does the amount of institutional grant reach a level where its elimination would wipe out the projected shortfall in institutional funds (approximately $2.3 million)? Only after the first 1011 students (just over 25% of the aided matriculants) had their aid eliminated and applied to the more needy students. What is the impact of the elimination of this aid on the families and its replacement with self help as suggested? This plan represents approximately $2,300 of aid per student converted from institutional grant to self help, and a financing plan for approximately $16,300 of parental contribution at the parent's discretion.

PMU's current prepayment plans apply only to families who receive no need-based financial aid. That is, families are not allowed to prepay the family contribution (neither the parental contribution nor the student contribution). At least this is in part because financial aid funds vary year by year (the awards are only annual), and calculation of financial need (and family contribution, the balance) is also done on an annual basis. Accepting prepayment for all four years of matriculation assumes that conditions will stay stable, and some of these conditions (government policy and family circumstance) are well beyond the control of the university.

If PMU *did* accept prepayment for these 1011 lower-need students, their total family contribution would be on average $18,238 for the first year of attendance, calculated as follows:

Original Parent Contribution	+	Original Student Contribution	+	Reduced Institutional Aid	=	Total Family Contribution
$13,189	+	$2,733	+	$2,316	=	$18,238

By prepaying their family contribution for all four years at the first year's rate ($18,238 x 4 = $72,952), the typical family would save $6,832 over what they would have to pay each year assuming a 6% annual increase in price (reasonable for PMU). If the family financed that amount over ten years, the monthly payment would be $964 starting immediately upon matriculation. Of course, if some savings was available the entire prepayment would not need to be financed and the monthly payments would be reduced. The risk to the institution is that the actual price will rise at a rate higher than the rate of return on the investment of the prepaid amounts. However, if the investment returns even 5.15% annually (almost a full point below the 6% increase in price) the institution will break even.

PMU's families are already comfortable with back-end financing as it applies to their prepayment plans, and there are already both the administrative mechanisms within the institution, as well as the relationships with a variety of lending institutions which would jump at the chance to offer loans to PMU's families at favorable terms. By extending the prepayment plans to aided families, in this case the least needy 25% of their families likely to be most sensitive to price, PMU can secure their attendance as well as divert their institutional grant funds to the most needy to try to bridge the gap between available and needed financial aid funds.

This analysis takes a most extreme position—reducing institutional grants as much as possible to balance the financial aid budget. The biggest risk is that even as the data show that these price sensitive students seem to matriculate even though their self-help is high, an additional $2,316 of obligation may be more than they can bear. If parental, rather than student, contribution is the real determining factor in their sensitivity to price, the availability of this new program may lessen the sting of the family contribution on the family's cash flow enough to overcome the additional obligation. Of course, PMU may be able to redirect the institutional grant of a smaller proportion of low-need students and balance the financial aid shortfall in other ways.

Conclusion

Colleges and universities have two major ways to span the growing gap between available funds and current program needs. First, they can try to contain costs by re-engineering both the administrative and academic processes on campus. Radical change in the way colleges and universities do business should yield some of the cost savings necessary to support the academic programs they wish to maintain. Second, academic institutions need to find new ways of leveraging the complex financial services activities they already perform to support their missions to their fullest.

Price discounts are a major way colleges and universities attract the students they want, and it is no surprise that less and less funding is available to support financial aid, the major form of price discounting. This study has developed a model of price sensitivity that any college or university can use to understand the characteristics of its own admitted and matriculating students. The study suggests strategies for maximizing the funds available for price discounts, as well as new and better ways of discounting the price of attendance. Sample data offered in this study from three institutions of very different types—a private multiversity, a private liberal arts college, and a public comprehensive university—showed that price sensitivity *does* exist in all these institutions. Additional research showed that the most complex of these institutions, the private multiversity, had already implemented some new mechanisms for price discounting (like tuition prepayment plans), but that its current and projected needs for funds available for discounting are forcing it to consider more innovative ways of offering financial aid.

The Academic Bank offers colleges and universities the opportunity to examine their financial needs comprehensively, and develop the right solutions based on those needs. The Academic Bank also offers colleges and universities a stable mechanism and structure for dealing with an increasing volatile financial services world. What should an institution do in order to benefit from these ideas?

1. Analyze its current student financing programs and project their funding requirements for at least five years.
2. Use the models presented in Chapters 2 and 3 of this study to determine how sensitive their students are to price.
3. Use the models presented in chapters 4 and 5 of this study to identify and document the current Academic Bank activities that are performed at the institution and look for ways to leverage them against one another.
4. Decide whether the creation of an Academic Bank is necessary, appropriate and feasible. If so, be creative, as Chapter 6 exemplified, in looking for solutions that combine reasonable goals for revenue generation to meet financial aid requirements with an acute understanding of the impact of these solutions on students and their behavior.

Notes

1. "On Need-Blind Admissions Policy: Role and Implications (The 1991-92 Report of the Council Committee On Undergraduate Admissions and Financial Aid)," (PMU [institutional identity protected]: 30 July 1992), p. I.

2. Many of these ideas were suggested and developed with assistance from the Office of Student Financial Services at PMU.

References

"8 Issues Affecting Higher Education: a Roll Call of the States." *Chronicle of Higher Education Almanac*. 28 August 1991.

"9 Issues Affecting Higher Education: a Roll Call of the States." *Chronicle of Higher Education Almanac*. 6 September 1989.

"9 Issues Affecting Higher Education: a Roll Call of the States." *Chronicle of Higher Education Almanac*. 5 September 1990.

"9 Issues Affecting Higher Education: a Roll Call of the States." *Chronicle of Higher Education Almanac*. 26 August 1992.

"9 Issues Affecting Higher Education: a Roll Call of the States," *Chronicle of Higher Education Almanac*. 25 August 1993.

"9 Issues Affecting Higher Education: a Roll Call of the States," *Chronicle of Higher Education Almanac*. 1 September 1994.

"America's Best Colleges: A New Era on Campus." *U.S. News and World Report*. 16 October 1989.

Anderson, Richard E. "Doing Good and Doing Well: A Review of the Entrepreneurial Activities of Colleges and Universities." *Capital Ideas*. 5(1 & 2). New York: National Center for Postsecondary Governance and Finance. June, 1990.

Anderson, Richard E. "Establishing a Financial Intermediary for College Savings." Unpublished Paper. February, 1989.

Anderson, Richard E. *Tuition Prepayment Guide*. College Park, MD: National Center for Postsecondary Governance and Finance, 1989.

"Appropriations Bill Would Deny Pell Grants to Some Part-Time Students After January 1." *Chronicle of Higher Education*, 18 October 1989.

Baldridge, J. Victor et al. *Policy Making and Effective Leadership*. San Francisco: Jossey-Bass, 1983.

Barrett, Paul M. "U.S. Investigates Prestigious Universities, Colleges for Possible Antitrust Violations." *Wall Street Journal*. August 10, 1989.

Baum, Sandy. "The Need for College Savings." in *College Savings Plans: Public Policy Choices*. Janet S. Hansen, ed. New York: The College Board, 1990.

Breneman, David W. and Susan C. Nelson. *Financing Community Colleges: An Economic Perspective*. Washington, D.C.: Brookings Institution, 1981.

Burkins, Glenn. "Look at Who's in the Financial-Services Business Now." *The Philadelphia Inquirer*. 15 July 1990.

"Bush Proposes the Creation of Family Savings Account." *Wall Street Journal*. 29 January 1990.

Calvert, Scott. "After Overlap, Financial Aid Changes." *The Summer Pennsylvanian*. July 23, 1992.

Carnegie Commission on Higher Education. *A Classification of Institutions of Higher Education*. New York: McGraw-Hill, 1973.

Collison, Michele N-K. "More Freshman Say They Are Choosing Colleges Based on Cost." *The Chronicle of Higher Education*, 22 January 1992.

Cook, John A. and Robert Wool. *All You Need to Know About Banks*. New York: Bantam, 1983.

Cooper, Kerry and Donald R. Fraser. *Banking Deregulation and the New Competition in Financial Services.* Cambridge, MA: Ballinger Publishing, 1984.

"Counting on Savings." editorial. *Wall Street Journal.* 19 January 1990.

"Double Trouble." *Policy Perspectives.* 2(1). Philadelphia: University of Pennsylvania, September 1989.

Dresang, Joel. "Pay Now, Learn Later—At Today's Rate." *USA Today.* 22 May 1989.

Dunn, John A. and Dawn G. Terkla. "When is it Going to Stop?: A Speculation on Tuition Rates at One Private University." *Proceedings of the NEAIR 15th Annual Conference.* Providence: Northeast Association of Institutional Research, October 1988.

El-Khawas, Elaine. "Campus Trends, 1992." *Higher Education Panel Report Number 82.* Washington, D.C.: American Counsel on Education, July 1992.

Feldman, Sheldon and Kimberly A. Reiley. *A Compilation of Federal and State Laws Regulating Consumer Financial Services.* West Lafayette, IN: Purdue Research Foundation, 1977.

Finn, Jr., Chester E. *Scholars, Dollars & Bureaucrats.* Washington, D.C.: The Brookings Institution, 1978.

Giddy, Ian H. "Is Equity Underwriting Risky for Commercial Bank Affiliates?" in *Deregulating Wall Street: Commercial Bank Penetration of the Corporate Securities Market.* Ingo Walter, ed. New York: John Wiley & Sons, 1985.

Gladieux, Lawrence E. and Gwendolyn L. Lewis. *The Federal Government and Higher Education: Traditions, Trends, Stakes and Issues.* New York: The College Board, 1987.

Hart, Natala K. "How Families Are Saving for College: What Market Surveys Tell Us." in *College Savings Plans: Public Policy Choices.* Janet S. Hansen, ed. New York: The College Board, 1990.

Patrick Healy, "IRS Abandons Attempt to Tax Michigan's Prepaid-Tuition Plan," *Chronicle of Higher Education.* 19 May 1995.

"Higher Education's New Majority." *Policy Perspectives.* 2(2). Philadelphia: University of Pennsylvania, January 1990.

Huertas, Thomas F. Comment on Thomas A. Pugel and Lawrence J. White, "An Analysis of the Competitive Effects of Allowing Commercial Bank Affiliates to Underwrite Corporate Securities" in *Deregulating Wall Street: Commercial Bank Penetration of the Corporate Securities Market,* Ingo Walter, ed., New York: John Wiley & Sons, 1985.

Jacobson, Robert L. "Academic Leaders Predict Major Changes for Higher Education in Recession's Wake." *Chronicle of Higher Education.* 20 November 1991.

Knapp, Laura Greene. "Update-Trends in Student Aid: 1981 to 1991." Washington, D.C.: The College Board, August 1991.

Leslie, Larry L. and Paul T. Brinkman. "Student Price Response in Higher Education: The Student Demand Studies." *Journal of Higher Education.* 58(2). 1987.

Lewis, Gwendolyn L. "Trends in Student Aid: 1980 to 1988." *Proceedings of the NEAIR 15th Annual Conference.* Providence: Northeast Association for Institutional Research, October 1988.

Lewis, Mervyn and Kevin Davis. *Domestic and International Banking.* Cambridge, MA: MIT Press, 1987.

Manual of the Counsel of Ivy Presidents, *Section X: Admissions and Financial Aid,* revised 11/87.

Massy, William F. "A Strategy for Productivity Improvement in College and University Academic Departments." Paper Presented at the *Forum for Postsecondary Governance*. Santa Fe, NM, 30 October 1989.

Massy, William F. "Productivity Improvement Strategies for College and University Administration and Support Services." Paper Presented at the *Forum for College Financing*. Annapolis, Md., 26 October 1989.

McDuff, Nancy G. "Financing the Costs of Higher Education: Planning Creative Student and Institutional Options." *Planning for Higher Education*. 18(1). Ann Arbor, MI: Society for College and University Planning, 1989.

McPherson, Michael S. and Morton Owen Schapiro. *Keeping College Affordable: Government and Educational Opportunity*. Washington, D.C.: Brookings Institution, 1991.

Mitgang, Lee. "Elite Colleges Pull Back from Guaranteed Student Aid." *Philadelphia Inquirer*. December 24, 1991.

Muffett, Diane, Marvin Smith, and Lee Gordon. "The Parents' Perspective on Financing Their Child's College Education." Research Report. West Lafayette, IN: Purdue University Division of Financial Aid, 1989.

"National Prepaid-Tuition Program is Started by Company Representing 14 Private Colleges." *Chronicle of Higher Education*. 25 October 1989.

Nazario, Sonia L. "Funding Cuts Take a Toll at University," *Wall Street Journal*. 5 October 1992.

Newman, Wes and Boll Ignelzi. "Selecting a Campus-Wide Card System." Durham, N.C.: Duke University, 1990.

Nicklin, Julie L. and Goldie Blumenstyk. "Number of Non-Teaching Staff Members Continues to Grow in Higher Education." *Chronicle of Higher Education*, 6 January 1993.

"On Need-Blind Admissions Policy: Role and Implications (The 1991-92 Report of the Council Committee On Undergraduate Admissions and Financial Aid)." PMU [institutional identity protected], 30 July 1992.

"Personal Savings Rate May Finally Recover." *Wall Street Journal.* 2 November 1992.

Prospectus: Registered Education Savings Plan. Toronto: University Scholarships of Canada, 1992.

Pugel, Thomas A. and Lawrence J. White. "An Analysis of the Competitive Effects of Allowing Commercial Bank Affiliates to Underwrite Corporate Securities" in *Deregulating Wall Street: Commercial Bank Penetration of the Corporate Securities Market.* Ingo Walter, ed. New York: John Wiley & Sons, 1985.

Pulliam, Susan. "Life Insurance Firms Plan to Pass Along Big Tax Increases to their Policyholders." *Wall Street Journal.* 10 December 1990.

Putka, Gary. "Group of Educators Backs Tuition-Prepayment Plan." *Wall Street Journal.* 18 July 1989.

Quint, Michael. "Bank Ties Savings Plan to Rise in College Costs." *New York Times.* 21 September 1987.

RESP Facts: University Scholarships of Canada Answer Your Questions About Saving for Your Child's Education. Toronto: University Scholarships of Canada, n.d.

Rose, Peter S. *The Changing Structure of American Banking.* New York: Columbia University Press, 1987.

"Save America: A Primer on U.S. Savings and Its Effect on Economic Health." Washington, D.C.: Institute for Research on the Economics of Taxation, May 1989.

Shea, Christopher "Many Private Colleges Curb Tuition Growth, but Increases Still Outpace Inflation," *Chronicle of Higher Education.* 17 March 1993.

Shultz, Ellen E. "College Savings Plans That May Not Make the Grade." *Wall Street Journal.* 4 November 1991.

"State Notes." *Chronicle of Higher Education.* 12 August 1992.

"State Notes." *Chronicle of Higher Education.* 15 April 1992.

"The 1980s: A Financial Retrospective." *Policy Perspectives.* 2(1). Philadelphia: University of Pennsylvania, September 1989.

"The Nation: Resources," *Chronicle of Higher Education Almanac.* 5 September 1990.

"The Nation: Resources," *Chronicle of Higher Education Almanac.* 28 August 1991.

"The Nation: Resources," *Chronicle of Higher Education Almanac.* 26 August 1992.

"The Nation: Resources," *Chronicle of Higher Education Almanac.* 25 August 1993.

"The Nation: Resources," *Chronicle of Higher Education Almanac.* 1 September 1994.

Tierney, Michael L. "The Impact if Financial Aid on Student Demand for Public/Private Higher Education." *Journal of Higher Education.* 51(5). 1980.

United States of America v. Brown University *et al.*, 91-CV-3274, "Final Judgement." 19 September 1991.

United States of America v. Brown University *et al.* 91-CV-3274. "Government's Motion for Summary Judgement." 3 April 1992.

United States of America v. Brown University *et al.* 91-CV-3274. "Government's Statement of Principal Factual Issues for Litigation." 20 April 1992.

United States of America v. Brown University *et al.* 91-CV-3274. "Massachusetts Institute of Technology's Pretrial Memorandum." 22 May 1992.

United States of America v. Brown University *et al.* 91-CV-3274. "Memorandum of Law in Support of Government's Motion for Summary Judgement." 3 April 1992.

"U.S. Roll Call: Prepaid-Tuition Plans." *Chronicle of Higher Education Almanac*. 1 September 1988.

"U.S. Roll Call: Tax-Exempt Bonds for College Savings." *Chronicle of Higher Education Almanac*. 1 September 1988.

Zemsky, Robert and Penney Oedel. *The Structure of College Choice*. New York: College Entrance Examination Board, 1983.

Index

Academic Bank, 17, 79, 81-82, 91-92, 97-110, 112, 115-116, 131-133, 137-138
affordability, 3, 45, 115, 131
aid, 3, 5, 8-11, 14-15, 17, 24-29, 32-47, 52, 55-56, 58-75, 77, 79, 92-93, 97-98, 101, 104-107, 110-111, 116-119, 121-122, 125-128, 130-131, 134-138
anti-trust, 26
applicant, 8, 24, 26-29, 33, 39-40, 52, 57, 74
assets, 10, 79-80, 84, 86, 91, 101, 106, 110
AT&T, 90
automated teller machines, 16, 122

bank, 13-18, 79-93, 97-98, 100, 103-104, 108-111, 115, 117, 121, 123, 129, 130-133
Bank Holding Company Act, 81, 86, 92
banking, *See bank*
Bechtle (Judge), 27
bond, 12-13
brokerage, 15, 80, 104, 106-109
Bush (George), 11

Canadian, 11, 108
COFHE, 29-32
College Board, 11, 27, 108
College Prepayment Fund, 12, 14

College Savings Bank, 11, 15, 108
CollegeSure CD, 11
commercial banks, 16, 82-83, 85-88, 90-91, 110-111, 121, 129
Congress, 8, 11, 29, 90
Congressional Methodology, 52
consumer credit companies, 88
consumer finance companies, 88
cost, 5-6, 13, 25, 46, 80, 82, 120, 137
credit cards, 16, 87-88, 122
credit union, 16, 83, 87-88, 91, 103, 110-111, 122, 132-133

debit and/or credit card, *See debit/credit card*
debit/credit card, 98, 107, 111-112, 122
default, 8, 16, 117
demand theory, 23-24, 33
deposit acceptance, 97, 103
Depository Institutions Deregulation and Monetary Control Act, 87, 89
deposit, 11, 15, 79, 83-86, 90-92, 97, 103, 105-107, 111
discount, 8, 13, 20, 34-35, 63, 97, 118, 120, 137
disintermediate, 15, 131
Duquesne University, 15

efficiency, 13, 23, 106, 120
electronic fund transfers, 79, 81
enrollment, 23-25, 33-34

149

equity, 15, 23, 86, 123, 126

family contribution, 9, 28, 97, 135-137
Family Savings Account, 11
Federal, 9, 13, 26, 85-89, 92, 99, 103-104, 109, 111, 132
Ford Motor Company, 88
foreign students, 119
fractional reserve banking, 80, 83

Garn-St Germain Act, 87, 89
General Electric, 90
General Motors, 15, 88
Glass-Steagall Act, 90
GMAC, 15, 90
government, 9, 11, 16-17, 23, 26-28, 45, 52, 83, 86-87, 92, 99, 101, 104, 108, 117, 119, 128-129, 135
grant 8-9, 26-27, 42, 45-46, 52, 65, 72, 98, 105-106, 110-111, 117-118, 122, 133, 135-137
GSL, *See Stafford*

HEMAR, 12, 14
Higher Education Act, 29

IBM, 90
Indiana, 101
industrial banks, 87
inflation, 3, 5-6, 9
insurance, 81-82, 85-86, 88-89, 91, 98, 108-110

intermediation, 17, 79-84, 88, 90-93, 97, 103-107, 110
intermediaries, 12, 14-15, 82, 91
Internal Revenue Service, 12, 99, 110, 112
investment banks, 89-90
investments, 9, 11-12, 14-15, 80, 87, 89, 97, 102, 104
IRS, *See Internal Revenue Service*
Ivy Overlap Group, *See Overlap*

Justice Department, 26

loans, 8-9, 15-16, 20, 52, 65, 83-91, 97-98, 104-106, 109-111, 117-118, 122-123, 126-129, 132-133, 135-136

market, 3, 7-8, 11, 15, 24, 36, 63, 85, 87-92, 102, 104-105, 112, 131
Michigan, 12
Minnesota, 12, 101
MIT, 26-28
money market, 87, 89
mortgage, 16, 122
mutual fund, 12, 80, 89-91, 108-110
mutual savings bank, 87, 110-111

NDSL, 52, 122, 128
need-blind, 25, 28-29, 37, 75, 77, 119

Overlap, 25-30, 33, 37, 51, 74, 118

Index

parental contribution, 14, 135
Parental Partnership, 133
Pell, 8, 45-46, 52
Pennsylvania, 13, 27, 33
PLA, 51-54, 56-61, 63-65, 67-75, 77
PMU, 51-53, 55-74, 77, 106, 115-137
portfolio transformation, 15, 80, 103, 105-106, 108-109
prepayment, 12-15, 102, 104, 108, 122-127, 134-137
price, 3-9, 11, 13-15, 17, 20, 23-30, 32-36, 38-45, 47, 49, 51-53, 55-56, 58-65, 70, 73-76, 79, 90-93, 97, 106, 108, 115-120, 123-127, 134, 136-138
price sensitive, *See price sensitivity*
price sensitivity, 7-8, 17, 24, 28-29, 33-36, 39-45, 47, 49, 51, 53, 56, 59, 73-76, 79, 91, 117, 123, 127, 134, 136-137
proprietary schools, 8
PUC, 51-52, 54-60, 62-73, 75, 77
Purdue University, 9, 101

quintile, 47, 59-71, 75

rating, 3

Registered Education Savings Plan (RESP), 11, 108
regulation, 5, 17, 81, 86-88, 99
Regulation Q, 89
revenue, 3, 5, 13-14, 23, 92, 99-100, 106, 111-112, 120-121, 138
risk, 81, 84-85, 90, 92, 100, 103, 105, 128, 132, 136

Sallie Mae, 110
save, 9-17, 27, 71-72, 86-89, 91-92, 97-98, 101-103, 108, 110-111, 117, 120, 131, 134, 136-137
saving, *See save*
Savings Bond, 102, 122
Securities and Exchange Commission (SEC), 12, 88
self help, 42-43, 45, 47, 65-72, 74-75, 134-135
SEOG, 45-46, 52, 135
Sherman Act, 27
simulation, 3, 6
SLS, 52, 77
Stafford, 8, 16, 46, 52, 104, 117-118, 122, 128-129
Stanford (University), 5
state, 6, 9-10, 12-14, 17, 23, 30, 32, 35, 45-46, 52, 56, 58-60, 62-73, 75, 77, 79-81, 83, 86-88, 90, 99, 101, 103-105, 108, 115, 119, 128, 131, 134
sticker price, 34
sticker shock, 7, 120
Supreme Court, 13

For Product Safety Concerns and Information please contact our EU
representative GPSR@taylorandfrancis.com
Taylor & Francis Verlag GmbH, Kaufingerstraße 24, 80331 München, Germany

www.ingramcontent.com/pod-product-compliance
Lightning Source LLC
Chambersburg PA
CBHW072219240426
43670CB00038B/2192